Waiting to Be Arrested at Night

A Uyghur Poet's Memoir of China's Genocide

Tahir Hamut Izgil

Translation and introduction by
JOSHUA L. FREEMAN

PENGUIN PRESS • NEW YORK • 2023

PENGUIN PRESS
An imprint of Penguin Random House LLC
penguinrandomhouse.com

"Memory of France" by Paul Celan, translated by Michael Hamburger,
reproduced with permission of Johnson & Alcock Ltd.

"The Women's Prison," "Road," "Your Unknown Place," "Body,"
"Somewhere Else," and "What Is It" were first published in *Asymptote*.

"Unity Road" and "Lost in Paris" originally appeared in *The Southern Review*.

Library of Congress Cataloging-in-Publication Data

Names: Izgil, Tahir Hamut, 1969– author. | Freeman,
Joshua L., translator, writer of introduction.
Title: Waiting to be arrested at night : a Uyghur poet's memoir of China's genocide /
Tahir Hamut Izgil ; translation and introduction by Joshua L. Freeman.
Description: New York : Penguin Press, 2023.
Identifiers: LCCN 2023009751 (print) | LCCN 2023009752 (ebook) |
ISBN 9780593491799 (hardcover) | ISBN 9780593491805 (ebook)
Subjects: LCSH: Izgil, Tahir Hamut, 1969– | Uighur (Turkic people)—
China—Xinjiang Uygur Zizhiqu—Biography. | Political
activists—China—Xinjiang Uygur Zizhiqu—Biography. |
Genocide—China—Xinjiang Uygur Zizhiqu. | Xinjiang Uygur Zizhiqu
(China)—Ethnic relations. | Xinjiang Uygur Zizhiqu (China)—Social conditions.
Classification: LCC DS731.U4 I974 2023 (print) |
LCC DS731.U4 (ebook) | DDC 323.151092 [B]—dc23/eng/20230321
LC record available at https://lccn.loc.gov/2023009751
LC ebook record available at https://lccn.loc.gov/2023009752

Printed in the United States of America
1st Printing

Designed by Alexis Farabaugh

When they search the streets and cannot find my vanished figure

Do you know that I am with you

PERHAT TURSUN, "ELEGY," 2006

Contents

Joshua L. Freeman

If you took an Uber in Washington, DC, a few years ago, there was a chance your driver was one of the greatest living Uyghur poets. Tahir Hamut Izgil arrived with his family in the United States in 2017, fleeing the Chinese government's merciless persecution of his people. Tahir's escape not only spared him near-certain internment in the camps that have swallowed more than a million Uyghurs; it also allowed him to share with the world his experiences of the calamity engulfing his homeland. This memoir is Tahir's firsthand account of one of the world's most urgent humanitarian crises, and of one family's survival.

Before I met Tahir, I knew his poems. I encountered them soon after I began working as a translator in Xinjiang, the Uyghur region in western China. A close friend there kept telling me that if I really wanted to understand Uyghur culture, I had to read the poetry. Like many Americans, I rarely felt drawn to poetry, and I paid little heed to my friend's advice. One day, though, another friend put a sheaf of Tahir's verses in my hand. Poetry had never affected me so deeply.

For Uyghurs, poetry is not merely the province of writers and intellectuals. Verse is woven into daily life—dropped into conversation, shared constantly on social media, written between lovers. Through poetry, Uyghurs confront issues as a community, whether debating gender roles or defying state repression. Even now, I wake up many mornings to an inbox full of fresh verse, sent by the far-flung poets of the Uyghur diaspora for me to translate.

Influence and eminence in the Uyghur community are often tied to poetry as well. Ask Uyghurs to name ten prominent Uyghurs, and several will be poets. Ask Uyghur intellectuals to name the most important Uyghur thinkers and writers, and the name Tahir Hamut Izgil might come up.

I met Tahir in early 2008, when I was beginning to translate Uyghur poetry. His presence was as memorable as his verse. Compact, energetic, and darkly handsome, Tahir had an intense gaze; his speech was forceful and precise. As our discussion ranged from poetry to politics to history to religion, the range of his interests and experiences became quickly apparent.

The son of dairy farmers, Tahir grew up in a village outside Kashgar, an ancient city in the southwest of the Uyghur region; the rhythms and folkways of Uyghur village life remain a wellspring for his poetry. He was born during the Cultural Revolution, at the height of Maoist radicalism, but came of age as an era of economic and cultural liberalization was dawning in the 1980s. The dreary, politicized poetry of the

Mao years was giving way to an efflorescence of new genres, styles, and themes. When Tahir published his first poem, while still in high school, he was joining a literary scene very much in ferment.

An excellent student, Tahir moved to Beijing for college. Coming from the Uyghur-speaking world of Kashgar, Tahir now strove to master Mandarin, working through volumes of Chinese avant-garde poetry alongside Chinese translations of Freud. Before long, he was reading widely in Western literature; for a time, the Chinese edition of Wallace Stevens's selected poems rarely left his side. It was a heady time, as he and other Uyghur students in Beijing formed groups to discuss their reading and push forward in their own literary efforts.

It was also a tumultuous period in China's capital. A new generation, unwilling to accept the tepid pace of reform, was increasingly demanding democratic rights and an end to corruption. As a sophomore, Tahir helped organize hunger strikes and marches by Uyghur students in the weeks leading up to the 1989 Tiananmen protests. While the student movement was ultimately crushed by Beijing's tanks, Tahir's interest in politics persisted.

Following college, Tahir worked for a time in Beijing before taking a position teaching Mandarin in Urumchi, capital of the Uyghur region. All the while, he continued writing poetry, much of it in a modernist vein, some of it dealing with subjects previously taboo in Uyghur literature. (One much-discussed 1994 poem touched on marijuana, masturbation, and "a nation turned into a drunkard.") Tahir increasingly gained a reputation in avant-garde circles as a talented young poet.

In 1996, the political realities of Uyghur life in China intruded.

Having left Urumchi with the hope of studying abroad, Tahir was arrested at the border while attempting to leave China. After confessing under torture to spurious charges of intent to expose state secrets, Tahir was imprisoned for nearly three years. Conditions were harsh, and his weight fell below a hundred pounds.

After his release in late 1998, Tahir was faced with beginning his life again, now with a black mark against his name in the party archive. The following year, he began working in film production, and was soon directing independent films. By the early 2000s, Tahir had established himself as a significant and highly original director, best known for his pathbreaking drama *The Moon Is a Witness*. His poetic work continued apace, as did his vast and varied reading.

It was a remarkable second act for a man who had emerged from a labor camp only a few years before, and it unfolded against a backdrop of deteriorating political conditions and ethnic relations in the Uyghur region. Over the course of the 2000s, the Chinese government largely eliminated the Uyghur-language education system and began forcing Uyghur children into Chinese-language boarding schools. Discrimination against Uyghurs by members of China's Han majority grew pervasive; Uyghurs seeking jobs were often told outright by potential employers that "we don't need minorities." Citing the unemployment problem created in part by its own policies, the government began pressuring Uyghurs to take low-wage jobs elsewhere in China, where they lived in crowded dormitories under strict supervision, surrounded by an unfamiliar and often unwelcoming society.

Year after year, Uyghur resentment festered, with no outlet for expression in the tightly controlled media. Finally, in mid-2009, after Han employees at a toy factory in eastern China lynched Uyghur colleagues following unfounded rumors of rape, Urumchi exploded in successive waves of violence between Uyghurs and Han. The death toll climbed into the hundreds as buses burned, shop windows were smashed, and passersby were bludgeoned to death in the streets.

In September, amid mass protests against the region's party secretary, Tahir was crossing a crowded street when several Han protesters suddenly shouted out to him, "Are you a Uyghur?" In his own homeland, Tahir later told me, he couldn't imagine denying who he was. "Yeah, I'm a Uyghur," he shouted back. "What's it to you?" Blows rained down on Tahir until he vaulted over a guardrail to safety. His eye still twitches sometimes from the beating, but the incident didn't slow him down.

I asked Tahir once if his resilience stemmed from his years in prison and in the labor camp. He said he didn't think so. Even before his imprisonment, he told me, he had known that being a Uyghur intellectual in China meant taking on certain risks.

I do think that his experiences helped Tahir see what was coming earlier than most. One night in autumn 2016, I had dinner with Tahir and several other friends. We had been having these dinners for nearly a decade, and as always, the toasts and jokes and debates continued late into the night. We lined the empty wine bottles up in a row as we savored the steaming horsemeat and noodles. Smoke lingered in the air as the novelist Perhat Tursun punctuated his famous anecdotes with long drags on his cigarette.

Afterward, Tahir offered to drive me home, and we walked out to his car in the dark. Instead of driving, though, we kept talking, sitting in his Buick in the empty parking lot. In a city where the walls have ears, this was a good place for a private conversation.

We discussed the worsening political situation in the Uyghur region. Gesturing to a newly built police station at the edge of the parking lot, Tahir told me that most of his fellow inmates from the labor camp had been questioned in recent months by the police. We talked about Tahir's recent trips abroad, and he asked me in some detail about life in the United States. I sensed that it was time for me to ask about something we had never discussed before. "Are you thinking about moving to America?"

He looked me straight in the eyes. "Yes, I am."

Tahir and his wife, Marhaba, were still struggling with the idea. Starting over in a new country and a new language wasn't an easy thing for a couple in their forties with two children, Tahir told me. They would have to leave behind their careers and their friends. And for the foreseeable future there would be no going back: once they had requested asylum in the United States, any return to China would carry the distinct possibility of imprisonment. Given the bleak political outlook in Xinjiang, however, Tahir and his family felt they should be prepared to leave if things got worse.

They got worse. Half a year later, as spring turned to summer, reports of mass arrests and internment camps began trickling out of the Uyghur region. Although I had left Xinjiang in late 2016, I could see for myself that the situation was serious. One by one, even my closest friends in the region began deleting me from their WeChat contacts, as communication with individuals abroad became a pretext for arrest.

Tahir remained in touch longer than most, writing from time to time to discuss my translations of his poetry, until his messages likewise trailed off. In late June 2017, though, he sent me a voice message. "In May the weather here got really bad," he told me, using the typical Uyghur circumlocution for political repression. "I had no chance to contact you. It was extremely hard for us, with the weather changing constantly." We exchanged a few messages about one of his poems.

And then, silence. Those were the last messages I ever received from any of my friends in the Uyghur region.

In the months that followed, the news from Xinjiang grew ever darker. It was clear that this was not, as many of us had hoped, just another passing campaign. As the dimensions of the crisis came into focus, I thought constantly about everyone I knew there. I worried in particular about Tahir, given his past as a political prisoner. But I had no way to know if he was all right; I had no way to know if anyone was all right.

The Uyghur region was now a gigantic prison, blanketed with security forces and a biometric surveillance system unique in human history. Villages and neighborhoods grew deserted as countless thousands were packed off to internment camps. Uyghurs' passports were confiscated, communications with the outside world cut off. Exit became all but impossible.

But in at least one case, the impossible came to pass. In late August, I received word from a mutual acquaintance in Shanghai that Tahir was preparing to leave for the United States. I held my breath, not daring to contact him till he was safely out of China. Then another mutual friend gave me an American phone number and told me it was Tahir's. I called.

Tahir picked up. *Tinchliqmu?* "How have you been?" We greeted each other as usual. Then I asked where he was. When he replied that he was in Washington with his family, relief washed over me. After months of relentlessly grim news from the Uyghur region, this felt like a miracle.

Not long after his arrival in the United States, Tahir began thinking about writing a personal account of the Xinjiang crisis. For the next few years, though, the challenges of putting down roots in a new country were all-consuming. He drove an Uber, took English classes, applied for asylum. Only in late 2020 did Tahir's circumstances permit him to start setting down in writing the memories that had been with him since his escape from China.

Once Tahir began composing his account, it poured out of him. He wrote as fast as I could translate; each time we discussed his drafts, new details and topics emerged. In summer 2021, *The Atlantic* published a section of Tahir's memoir in condensed form. Meanwhile, the crisis in Xinjiang continued. Tahir kept writing.

The memoir that follows comprises one man's recounting of the destruction of his homeland. While composing it, Tahir spoke widely with others in the refugee community and checked his recollections against personal records and public sources. Aside from his immediate family and a few other individuals, he altered names and identifying details to protect those mentioned from state retribution.

Among the galaxy of talented Uyghur writers in Xinjiang, Tahir is, to my knowledge, the only one who has escaped China since the mass internments began. His account combines a poet's power of expression with a clear eye for the moral ambiguity found in even the most extreme circumstances. While the system of state terror in Xinjiang is orchestrated by an inhuman bureaucracy, the individuals running that system—and those crushed by that system—are human in full, and their complexity is present throughout Tahir's narrative.

The world revealed by that narrative is one we all must grapple with. The Chinese government's war on its Uyghur minority is unprecedented, but the tools it employs are familiar. State repression in Xinjiang relies on weaponized social media, computer algorithms that monitor and predict behavior, and an array of high-tech surveillance technology, much of it developed in the West. Islamophobic discourses that gathered strength in the United States have been central to China's efforts to justify its Xinjiang policies, while international corporations have been implicated in supply chains reaching back to forced labor in the Uyghur region.

Along with Tahir, my longtime circle of friends in Urumchi included various other individuals who populate this memoir, a remarkable group of writers and intellectuals whose voices still echo in my mind. The richness and vibrancy of this milieu can be glimpsed even amid the tragedy coursing through these pages: the shopkeeper lovingly translating Bertrand Russell even as the threat of arrest draws closer; the novelist whose irrepressible sense of humor leavens the unfolding atrocity.

Every one of these individuals could testify eloquently to the ongoing crisis—if they could speak to us. But they cannot: the persecution of the past several years has silenced their voices, at least for now. It is for them, and for countless unknown others, that Tahir shares his story with the world.

Waiting to Be
Arrested at Night

The Interrogation

After lunch on a March day in 2009, I was sitting in my library reading. My wife, Marhaba, was in the kitchen putting away dishes.

Someone knocked at the door. I opened it to find two young Uyghur men and a young Uyghur woman. Behind me, Marhaba stepped out of the kitchen.

"Are you Tahir Hamut?" asked the young man standing in front.

"I am."

"We wanted to talk with you about your household registration. Would you mind coming with us to the police station?" His voice was calm. The pair behind him seemed to be his assistants. It was clear that my guests were plainclothes police officers.

In China, a household registration records basic information about each member of a family, and is considered the most important form of identifying document. Examining a household registration is a frequent excuse for police to inspect a house or detain an individual.

"Of course," I responded, equally calm.

"Bring your ID card with you," the officer added.

"I've already got it." I patted the wallet in my pocket.

Marhaba watched us nervously.

"Don't worry, it's nothing," I said to her as I put on my jacket and shoes. "It's just about our household registration."

As we headed downstairs, I noticed that the officers walked before and behind me, hemming me in. The weather was clear but cold.

They had come in a civilian car, which meant that all of this was happening off the books. I sat in the back with the young man who had spoken with me. The other man drove; the young woman sat in the passenger seat.

Naturally, I wondered why they had taken me. I couldn't think of anything I had done recently that could have been the cause.

We drove out of our apartment complex and were soon on the main road. To reach our local police station, we needed to turn left at the intersection. We turned right. Just then, the young man who had spoken to me fished his police ID out of his pocket and held it up to me casually.

"My name is Ekber. This is Mijit. We're from the Urumchi Public Security Bureau. We wanted to chat with you a bit." He didn't introduce the young woman.

It was a good sign that Ekber had addressed me by the respectful pronoun *siz*. If they considered me a criminal, they would have curtly used the informal *sen* right from the start.

I remained silent and did my best to maintain my composure. In my experience, reacting too strongly was unhelpful in these situations. It was important that I give the impression I had no idea why I had been taken. They enjoyed seeing people's fear, anxiety, and confusion.

"What do you do for a living?" asked Ekber. This wasn't an interrogation; he was testing me.

"I'm a film director." I kept my reply simple.

He nodded in acknowledgment and continued his questioning. "Do you write screenplays as well?"

Hearing this, I wondered if they had detained me on account of my writing.

"No, I direct other people's screenplays."

"Whose screenplays have you directed?"

I mentioned three authors' names. One of them was my friend Perhat Tursun.

"Perhat Tursun—is he the one who insulted our Prophet Muhammad?"

I was shocked to hear something like this from a police officer, but I quickly collected myself. He must be trying to get a sense of my religious views. Still, I was irked by his comment.

"Have you read the novel in which Perhat Tursun supposedly insulted the Prophet?" My voice betrayed my irritation.

He wasn't ready to back down. "No, I read the essay written about the novel."

"I'd suggest you give the novel a read," I retorted. "You government employees need to be thorough."

Published ten years earlier, Perhat Tursun's *The Art of Suicide* dealt with themes that Uyghur literature had customarily avoided: alienation, sexuality, suicide. With its challenge to Uyghur aesthetic conventions and social mores, the novel had made waves on the literary scene. Following one conservative critic's false accusation that the novel insulted the Prophet, Perhat Tursun was widely attacked amid fierce public debate. Some even threatened his life.

"Are you also a writer?" asked Ekber.

"I write poetry."

"What kind of poems do you write?"

"You wouldn't understand the kind of poems I write."

"Ah, you write that murky abstract stuff?" He grinned mockingly. I said nothing. It was silent in the car. We drove along familiar city streets.

I still didn't know why the police had taken me today, and wondered if it was related to my time in prison a dozen years earlier. If so, I had a big problem.

In 1996, I had planned to go study in Turkey, and had been arrested at China's border with Kyrgyzstan for "attempting to take illegal and confidential materials out of the country." In an era when any Uyghur could be arrested under any pretext, my turn had come. After a year and a half in an Urumchi prison, I was sentenced to three years of reform through labor. Having already served half of that time, I was sent to serve the remaining year and a half of my sentence in the Kashgar Re-education Through Labor Camp.

By the time I was released from the camp, I had already been fired from my job as a teacher. I returned to Urumchi with no job, no money, no home; all I had was my household registration.

Working day and night, I managed to gain a foothold as a film director. As a "barefoot director," though, working outside the state system, I was mostly hired to direct low-budget television series, music videos, and advertisements. I made barely enough to support myself. Sometimes I couldn't even find a film to direct.

Around that time, Xinjiang Television Station was hiring translators to render the Chinese-language daily news into Uyghur. Although I scored first on the proficiency test among the three hundred or so applicants, the political background check revealed that I had previously been fired from my job. The television station rejected my application.

After that, I worked for a time as a writer. I found it impossible, though, to make a living through writing. That was where things stood when Marhaba and I got married in 2001.

We had met quite a few years earlier, after I returned from Beijing to work in Urumchi. Perhat Tursun had been working after hours at a small company that provided agricultural information to Uyghur farmers, and he invited me to join him. Since I wasn't teaching many courses at the school where I worked, I agreed. It was at this company that I first met Marhaba, who had also only recently started working there. I often caught this clever-looking girl glancing at me, taking my measure.

She was five years younger than me, and by custom should have called me Tahir *aka*. The word *aka*, meaning older brother, is typically used by Uyghurs to respectfully address any older male. Older females are addressed as *hede*, or older sister. But Marhaba just called me Tahir. I could tell there was something special about her.

While we were working at the agricultural information firm, we would sometimes get lunch together, and we chatted often. We gradually grew closer.

During the three years I spent in prison, I lost all contact with Marhaba. When I returned to Urumchi after my release, one of the first things I did was confirm with Perhat's wife that Marhaba was still single. A few days later, Marhaba and I decided to meet in front of People's Theater.

When I arrived, I saw her there waiting. She looked at me with the sweetest smile. Once we had greeted each other, though, she grew troubled. Three years earlier, she had been deeply hurt when I left without saying goodbye. When she heard that I had been arrested, she cried for three days, not leaving her home. She couldn't eat.

On that frigid winter day, not long before nightfall, we stood talking by the road while cars whizzed by. Three years in prison had left me sensitive to everything, but after hearing her words I stopped noticing the cold.

After that, we saw each other regularly. Now that my years of misery had ended, I felt a powerful need for the warmth of a family, and my relationship with Marhaba gradually grew deeper. She was good-hearted and kind. She visited me often, looked after me, took my sorrows as her own.

Finally, the two of us decided to get married. My parents in Kashgar didn't have much, but they gave us money to rent an apartment. For the dowry, I borrowed five thousand yuan from a friend—a very small dowry. "Don't worry about it," Marhaba said. "If we work at it together, we can make money, we can have a good life." After we got married, Marhaba and I returned the five thousand yuan together.

Not long after we got married, we had to transfer our housing registrations to a combined listing in our new neighborhood. I went to the police station where I was registered, picked up my materials, and brought them to our new police station. The Han policewoman responsible for household registrations looked over my materials. Her curt reaction caught me off guard.

"Your current ID number is different from the ID number in your registration archive."

"How could they be different?"

"Your original ID number is a Beijing number, beginning with eleven," she replied briskly. "But your current ID number is an Urumchi number—it starts with sixty-five. This is wrong. Each person has only one ID number. Your Beijing number is the one that counts."

I was momentarily at a loss for words. "What should I do now?" I finally asked.

"Go to the police station that gave you the registration. Fix your ID number, and then come back. Otherwise your registration can't be moved here."

When I left for college in Beijing, I had taken my registration with me, as required by the government. Not long after, when China introduced the first generation of ID cards, I received a card; since my registration was in Beijing, my card bore a Beijing number. After I returned to Urumchi, I moved my registration to the local police station and received a new ID card with an Urumchi number. I paid no heed to the change; I assumed that when a registration is moved, the ID number must change as well. For six years, I had used this ID with no issue. Now, it turned out that this ID number was incorrect.

The next day I returned to the old police station and explained the situation. The Han police officer in charge of registrations glanced at the materials she had given me the previous day and saw the problem immediately. She just sat there, though, not saying anything. "Is it really incorrect?" I asked, wanting to be sure. Clearly, she didn't want to admit the error. Government officials, and particularly police officers, are reluctant to admit their mistakes. I thought the ID number had probably been changed six years earlier by a different officer, but if so, this policewoman was covering for that other officer, defending the honor of the whole system.

Suddenly she raised her head. "Why didn't you discover this problem at the time?"

"I assumed that when a registration was brought to Urumchi from elsewhere, the ID number changed."

"The error was yours," she said firmly.

I ran out of patience. "You did this incorrectly, and now you're blaming it on me? I can't change the ID number, this is completely your responsibility."

"That's not how it works," she said, ignoring what I had said. "Bring us a letter of apology, acknowledging that you are at fault for not discovering the problem in time. Then I'll process it for you."

There was nothing more to be said. I knew I should be pleased there was a means of resolving the issue, even at the cost of shouldering the guilt myself. After I wrote the letter of apology, the police officer filled out a form titled "Certification of Xinjiang Resident's ID Number Change." It stated that my current ID number was incorrect, and that my previous ID number would be restored. She stamped the form.

With the restoration of my old ID number, the previous six years of my life, including the three years I spent in prison, became a numberless life. In truth, this was a blessing for me. I hoped and believed that the record of my punishment and imprisonment had now been wiped from the police system. Networked computers had not yet been widely adopted.

When we got married, Marhaba and I had no steady employment, and made ends meet doing this and that. We both worked hard as we started our family; our days were long but happy. Eventually, I took a position directing films at a private media company. We had two kids. For seven years, we rented an apartment; finally, in 2008, we were able to take out a mortgage and buy our own place.

My work as a director was increasingly well-known. I continued writing verse and gained some reputation as a poet. After much effort and many setbacks, life for us had finally settled into a groove, and we felt a measure of stability.

In the ten years since my release from prison, the police had sought me out from time to time on various pretexts, as they did numerous other Uyghur intellectuals. These incidents, though, were never connected to my time in prison. In addition to my ID number having changed, I believe this was also due to the fact that I was arrested in Qizilsu Prefecture, while my household registration was in Urumchi. Unless it was a particularly important case, the police usually concerned themselves only with issues in their own precincts. It was not feasible for Qizilsu police officers to regularly travel the fifteen hundred kilometers to Urumchi to keep me under watch.

If my time in prison now caused the Urumchi police to add me to their blacklist, I would be under close surveillance for the rest of my life. My family's hard-won stability would be shattered.

We drove down a narrow downtown road and stopped in front of the Tengritagh District police station. It was an old building. The plainclothes officers led me into a nondescript office on the second floor. There were three tables and three chairs, with an unremarkable computer on each table. The tables and the computer screens were covered with a thin layer of dust; I figured it had been at least a month since anyone had been in the office.

Ekber gestured for me to take the chair closest to the door. The female officer had disappeared. "Would you like something to drink?" Ekber asked me.

"I'll have a Coke, if there is one," I replied.

Mijit left the office. Ekber switched on the computer by the window and addressed me politely. "May I see your ID card?" I removed my ID from my wallet and walked it over to him. He placed it on the table.

Mijit returned with three cold cans of Coca-Cola. He handed one to me and another to Ekber. Ekber left the room. Drinking my Coke, I did my best to appear calm. Mijit put his drink down on the table, looked for a moment at the flickering computer screen, and walked toward the door. Before he could leave, I told him I needed to use the restroom. I wanted to see their reaction. There was no one in the corridor; Mijit told me to follow him, and led me to a bathroom a couple of doors down. I stepped inside. Mijit followed me into the bathroom, watching me closely. Apparently, I was a person of considerable interest to them.

Returning to the office with Mijit, I resumed my seat. Mijit left the office.

They left me there alone for almost an hour. This was a psychological offensive. Anyone in my position would be anxious to know why they had been brought here; the longer they were left alone without any information, the more agitated, confused, and desperate they would become. Since I was aware of this, I managed to more or less keep my nerve.

Finally, Ekber and Mijit returned to the office. Mijit was carrying a packet of ruled paper and a pen. Ekber drew up a chair and sat across from me. Mijit took up a seat at the computer by the window.

Ekber began speaking. "Perhaps you haven't been somewhere like this before. I imagine you're rather nervous, but don't worry; there's nothing to be nervous about. We just had some questions for you. All you have to do is answer honestly and this will all be over."

As soon as I heard this, I understood that today's questioning had nothing to do with my time in prison. I relaxed considerably.

"Of course," I said with confidence.

Methodically and tirelessly, Ekber asked me at some length about my life and personal details: name, age, address, workplace, family members, relatives, brief biography, and more. This was a formality.

When giving my biography, I skipped over my time in prison. Speaking of the school that fired me, I said I had "resigned from my position." In the mid- and late 1990s it had been all the rage to "jump into the sea." Innumerable government cadres and employees in state-owned enterprises had given up their steady jobs to try their chances in the private sector. My comment about having resigned would attract no special notice.

Mijit wrote all of this down. As I was providing my basic information, he glanced several times at my ID card on the table.

As he wrote, Mijit's pen repeatedly gave him trouble. Again and again, he shook it to get the ink flowing. I began feeling bad for him. It was a shame I didn't have a pen to lend him, I thought. But his patience surprised me. Had I been in his place, I would have walked over to another office and found a better pen.

After obtaining my background information, Ekber asked what sort of work my company did. I began giving a detailed rundown of our operations.

"Does your company have any international contacts?" he inquired, his tone casual.

I understood at once. The key point had finally emerged: today's questioning concerned connections abroad.

"I think the daughter of one of our employees is studying abroad," I said earnestly.

"How about you? Do you have any connections abroad?" he inquired, drawing closer to the topic at hand.

"I'm in contact with two people abroad. My friend Jüret is studying for his doctorate in Japan, and we keep in touch on a regular basis. My friend Ablet is pursuing a PhD in Holland; we also talk often on the phone." As I said this, I recalled that a week ago Ablet and I had spoken on the phone for more than an hour. The reason for today's questioning was becoming clearer.

Ekber asked first about Jüret. This was another of his maneuvers as he closed in on the target. I decided to test him: because his objective was Ablet, I deliberately took my time as I described my relationship with Jüret. A close friend of mine since high school, Jüret had attended medical school in Chengdu, in Sichuan Province. After graduation, he returned to the Uyghur region, where he worked first at the Autonomous Region Uyghur Traditional Medicine Hospital and then at the Oncology Hospital, both of them located in Urumchi. I could see Ekber growing impatient as I prattled on in excruciating detail. When I reached Jüret's preparations for studying abroad in Japan, Ekber ran out of patience and interrupted me. "What about Ablet? What's your relationship with Ablet in Holland?"

We had finally gotten down to it. I spoke of how Ablet and I had long been close, about his work as an editor at an Urumchi publishing house, about his departure to study in Holland. Ekber asked when and why I had most recently spoken with him.

Ablet had phoned me around noon the Saturday before last. Ten days before, he had called to ask if I could send him some of my poems. His wife, having recently arrived in Holland from Urumchi, found herself with a good deal of time on her hands and was planning to translate some Uyghur poetry into English. After that conversation, I had sent

Ablet a dozen or so of my poems via email, but for some reason they hadn't reached him. This was what he had called to ask me about that Saturday. I promised to resend the poems to him shortly.

Ablet and I had then started discussing Uyghur intellectual life, and were deep in conversation when Marhaba gestured for me to get off the phone for lunch. I couldn't bear, though, to end the conversation with my friend on the other side of the world.

I described the phone call to Ekber in detail. Needless to say, there had been nothing in the call to attract the police's attention. Uyghur intellectuals typically exercised great care in what they said to each other over the phone; we often joked that we policed ourselves more than the police. It seemed to me that it must be the phone call's unusual length, rather than its content, that had come to the authorities' attention. The police wanted to know what a Uyghur living abroad and a Uyghur in Urumchi had discussed on an international phone call for more than an hour.

Ekber must have been satisfied with my detailed account. His expression grew noticeably more relaxed.

"I understand. That was what we had wanted to know." He smiled. "You also studied in Beijing. I'm a graduate of People's Public Security University."

"Is that so?" I returned his smile. At that moment, though, I saw Marhaba in my mind's eye, sitting anxiously back at home. I was suddenly consumed with the urge to be gone from this place. But Ekber showed no signs of hurrying.

"Of course, I'm a good deal younger. You are an *aka* to me. Now that we've had the chance to get acquainted, let's keep in touch."

This was the last thing I wanted to hear. I had no choice, though, but to assent.

"Of course," I replied warmly.

"We'll get in touch when we have the time. If I can't call you myself, Mijit will give you a ring. Let's have a nice chat over a meal."

This was a noose.

"Sure," I said boldly. "Call me whenever it's convenient."

"Oh, one other thing," added Ekber with a sudden look of seriousness. "What do you use to communicate online?"

"I just use email or QQ Messenger."

"The poems you sent Ablet must still be in your email?"

Ekber intended to test the truthfulness of what I had told him, and to see whether there were any political issues with those poems.

"I'm sure they must be."

"In that case, leave us your email address and QQ number as well as your passwords." Ekber's tone was brusque. "It's six p.m. now. For the next twenty-four hours, don't touch either account."

Mijit flipped to the last page of the report he had just finished. He placed it on the table in front of me and handed me his defective pen. I took the pen, shook it hard a couple of times, and wrote down the information Ekber had requested. Mijit handed my ID back.

As we walked out of the building, Ekber prepared to take his leave. "OK, then, Tahir *aka*, let's stay in touch." It struck me as thoroughly empty now for him to call me *aka*.

"How am I supposed to get home?" I asked in annoyance. "Since you all brought me here, perhaps you'll take me back?" After they had spent half the day questioning me with no justification, I had to get back a bit of my own.

Neither of them had expected me to say anything like that. Ekber was thrown a bit off-balance. Mijit shot him a glance.

"Ah, sure, sure." Ekber pulled himself quickly together. "Mijit will take you back. Marhaba *hede* must be waiting for you. Why don't you give her a call to ease her mind," he finished puckishly.

Mijit drove me back in the same car. By the time we reached our neighborhood it was already dark.

As soon as I walked in the door, Marhaba flung herself at me and burst into tears. She had been worried sick. Our daughters, Aséna and Almila, ran up and clung tightly to me.

After the police had taken me away, Marhaba had immediately begun calling friends and acquaintances, pleading for them to find help for me from anyone they knew on the police force. A couple of acquaintances had already begun making inquiries as to my whereabouts. I promptly called to tell them nothing serious had happened and that I was already home safe. I thanked them and hung up the phone.

The next evening, a couple of hours after Ekber's twenty-four-hour period had ended, I abandoned the email and QQ accounts I had given him and registered for new accounts. I decided that I would refrain for a while from contacting people abroad, including Ablet and Jüret.

Two weeks later, I was working in my office when Ekber called. After we exchanged pleasantries, he told me he would like to meet for a chat if I had time. I explained politely that I was exceedingly busy at the moment, that I would be free in a few days, and that we could meet up then to chat. If I could use excuses like this to avoid Ekber and Mijit, eventually I could break free of them altogether. If I met with them once, my troubles would never cease. They intended to exploit my fear of the police to see what they could get out of me. If things worked out as they hoped, they could press me to inform on people around me; at the very least, they could make me pick up the tab for meals.

A couple more weeks passed. Mijit called me, saying that Ekber wanted to talk. I quickly came up with another excuse: I was burning the candle at both ends to finish a documentary film and wouldn't be free for a while, but I'd call Ekber myself as soon as I had a spare moment. It seemed they weren't ready to let me go so easily.

Around that time, the Autonomous Region Department of Culture decided to organize a festival celebrating the distinctive culture of the Dolans, a Uyghur community living primarily in the southwest of our homeland. The festival would be held in Mekit, a county considered to be a center of Dolan culture, and a major arts performance was planned for the opening ceremony. To oversee the performance, the government appointed an executive director. He was an extremely busy man, so the organizers needed a managing director to take care of the day-to-day work, particularly during the lengthy preparations in Mekit preceding the festival. They asked me to take on the job.

I was in a taxi heading to the airport when Mijit called, once more asking to meet. Seeing an opportunity to finally slip free of the noose, I did not mince words. "I'm on my way to Mekit on government assignment for a month. I am not some idle person. You cannot simply keep bothering me like this." My tone was harsh as I drove the message home. "If I've committed a crime, arrest me. If not, stop with these tedious phone calls and absurd requests." I placed ostentatious emphasis on the fact that I was traveling for government work. To scare the government's men, you had to use the government. It was precisely people like me, working outside the government system, that they liked to bully.

It worked like a charm. They stopped contacting me.

In early May, a friend of mine got married at the Vineyard Restaurant in Urumchi. Practically all of my close friends and acquaintances in the city were there. As master of ceremonies, I spent the wedding running around taking care of various things.

At one point during the proceedings, I ducked into the restroom. When I emerged, I ran directly into Ekber. "Ah, have you come to the wedding, too?" I asked him without skipping a beat.

"Yes, I'm here for the wedding," he replied, clearly flustered. "I'll see you in a bit." He beat a hasty retreat into the bathroom.

Trying to figure out what Ekber was doing at the wedding, I walked over to the bride and groom's table and discreetly asked my friend whether a police officer named Ekber had been invited. He assured me no such person was on the guest list. My role in the ceremony provided a good pretext for me to take a turn around the hall, keeping a careful eye out for Ekber. He was nowhere to be found.

The groom had only recently returned from studying abroad, and an American friend of ours was among the guests. I assumed these to be the reasons for Ekber's uninvited appearance. It must be his responsibility to keep people with international connections under watch. Now, I understood, nowhere lay beyond the gaze of the secret police.

Although I knew we couldn't escape this kind of regular police harassment, and although I saw little reason to believe things would improve, I couldn't help hoping that I could somehow avoid going through all this again. I was so tired of living in fear.

ONE

A Phone Call from Beijing

I keep returning to the first day of 2013.

That evening, I received an unexpected call from Ilham Tohti, an economics professor at Beijing's Central University for Nationalities. It had been years since we'd talked. He was at a Uyghur restaurant behind the university, celebrating the new year over dinner with a mutual friend of ours from Beijing.

After exchanging pleasantries, Ilham declared: "Xi Jinping has taken power. Things will get better for us now. Don't lose heart, and let our friends in Urumchi know that they should feel optimistic." Ilham was in an excellent mood. When he said things would get better, he was referring to Uyghurs' rapidly deteriorating political circumstances.

While today it's clear how absurd it was to expect any good to come to Uyghurs from Xi Jinping, at the time numerous Uyghur intellectuals cherished such hopes. Some liberal Han intellectuals likewise suggested that Xi might turn out to be relatively liberal. Given the lack of transparency in Chinese politics, the political inclinations of new leaders were often subject to speculation.

Xi's father, Xi Zhongxun, had been the ranking Communist Party official in northwest China soon after the party took power, and had criticized repressive state policies in the Uyghur region. Uyghur intellectuals preferred to think that Xi Jinping would follow in his father's footsteps on the Uyghur issue. These were hopes born of desperation, a battered community's daydream of better treatment by its colonial rulers.

I had met Ilham Tohti in the early 1990s at Central University for Nationalities (as it was then known), where I was finishing my bachelor's degree and Ilham was studying for his master's in economics. Ilham was an immensely energetic and loquacious man; he spoke quickly, as if his head was packed with words and he was rushing to get them all out. When we ran into each other on campus, he would begin talking excitedly on the spot as professors and students passed by. Once Ilham got started, he was hard to stop, especially on his favorite topic, the economy and demography of the Uyghur region.

Ilham would go on to become perhaps the most prominent dissident Uyghur intellectual in China. In the mid-2000s he founded a Chinese-language website called Uyghur Online, where he published articles defending Uyghurs' legal rights. Ilham argued that the Chinese government's own autonomy policies were not being implemented in the Uyghur region; that the Production and Construction Corps in Xinjiang functioned as a lawless state within a state; that the rapid influx of Han settlers was making the region's indigenous communities into minorities in their own homeland; that Uyghurs faced crushing unemployment; that the Uyghur language had been marginalized in the educational system.

A central goal of Uyghur Online was encouraging healthy dialogue between Han and Uyghurs and strengthening interethnic understanding. The website became a hub for like-minded intellectuals and students—Uyghurs, Han, and others—and became increasingly influential abroad. My cousin had introduced me to Uyghur Online; he told me that numerous young Uyghurs had become active readers and that they often debated what they read on the site.

Needless to say, Ilham Tohti's dissenting views drew the attention of the Chinese government. The police regularly invited him to "tea," a euphemism for taking someone for an informal warning or questioning. During some sensitive periods, like the 2008 Beijing Olympics or visits by Western leaders to Beijing, police would take Ilham's family for a monthlong "vacation." In 2009, following the government's declaration that Ilham bore responsibility for the July violence in Urumchi, he and his family disappeared. People assumed Ilham had been arrested. But after a month and a half of informal detention in the Beijing suburbs, he and his family were allowed to return home.

Despite all this, Ilham never believed that the government would formally arrest or imprison him. He was, after all, a professor at a university in the national capital, and considered his vocal criticism to be entirely within the law. The fact that his household was registered in Beijing also lent him some peace of mind. But the political climate in the capital was very different from that in the Uyghur region. If Ilham had engaged in the same activities in Xinjiang, he would already have been arrested.

Things did not turn out as Ilham thought they would. In mid-January 2014, news of Ilham's arrest at his Beijing apartment reached us in Urumchi. When I heard the news, I inquired as to which police force had arrested him, and was told that the officers had arrived from Urumchi.

It was not normal for Urumchi police officers to travel more than two thousand kilometers to arrest a professor at a university in Beijing. Normally, if Ilham were to be arrested, the Beijing police would have jurisdiction. The involvement of the Urumchi police meant that Ilham's arrest was a decision made at the highest levels. Not long after, we learned that a number of Ilham's Uyghur students had disappeared from their school around the same time, likely into police custody. In other words, the situation was grave.

I was alarmed by the arrest of an intellectual who had merely called for the government to enforce its own laws. It gave me the sinking feeling that catastrophe lay ahead for Uyghur intellectuals as a group. As a measure against the approaching danger, I set aside time to review the files in my laptop as well as my desktop computer at work, and deleted every document, video, recording, and image that police could conceivably seize on as a pretext. I directed every employee in our office to conduct a similar "cleaning" of their own computer.

Not long before, while browsing the internet, I had come across "Charter 08," a manifesto in which the Nobel Prize–winning Han dissident Liu Xiaobo and others called for democracy and civil liberties in

China. After reading the manifesto, I decided to translate it into Uyghur; but, as I had no chance to publish the translation, it just sat on my computer. A couple of years earlier, a friend had given me a Word file with a Chinese translation of *Xinjiang: China's Muslim Borderland*, a collection of scholarly articles by more than a dozen specialists from the United States and elsewhere. The People's Liberation Army's political department had translated the book into Chinese, presumably for internal circulation. Given the tight state control over information from abroad, I was eager to get my hands on any foreign materials I could relating to Uyghurs and our homeland, and I read the book cover to cover at least three times. I also had a PDF of Han writer Wang Lixiong's book *My Western Regions, Your East Turkestan*, which had been published in Taiwan. And there was a photo that the Dalai Lama had taken with exiled Uyghur leader Rebiya Kadeer, his arm draped affectionately around her shoulder. I had been moved to see this warm connection between leaders of two communities facing oppression in China.

It had taken me a great deal of effort to find and translate these materials, and my unease grew as I reluctantly deleted them one by one. Later events, though, would prove this decision correct. Things were getting worse.

The repression following the 2009 violence in Urumchi had not yet concluded when the government began a separate campaign directed at Uyghurs. Known as "Strike Hard," this campaign was supposed to target "religious extremism, ethnic separatism, and violent terrorism," and its effects were far-reaching. Han migrants began arriving in Xinjiang in even greater numbers than before; Uyghurs' homes were demolished and their land confiscated. Uyghur religious practice and cultural life were increasingly suppressed, and Uyghurs faced ever-increasing discrimination in daily life. The problems Ilham Tohti had identified did not merely go unaddressed; they festered. Yet the government insisted that any Uyghur discontent stemmed from separatism and terrorism, and punished people indiscriminately.

Two months after Ilham Tohti's arrest, in March 2014, news came of a terrorist incident at a railway station in the southern Chinese city of Kunming, thousands of kilometers from Urumchi. State media announced that five black-masked Uyghurs had attacked people with knives in the ticket-sales hall.

Another two months passed. State media reported that two Uyghurs armed with knives had attacked passengers at the exit to the Urumchi train station before blowing themselves up. Not long after, it was reported that Uyghur terrorists had carried out a suicide attack on a morning market in Urumchi.

In the years immediately following the 2009 violence in Urumchi, the situation in the Uyghur region had seemed calmer. Now, with this spate of violent attacks in the space of three months, things once again grew tense. The government's posture and rhetoric became more aggressive than ever.

Uyghurs typically referred to such incidents by saying "Something's happened." People I knew had complex feelings about these events. On the one hand, their resentment toward the government and the Han made them feel on some level that it served them right. On the other hand, they felt it was wrong to target civilians rather than the government. In addition, people worried that such incidents would result in even more state repression that could personally harm them. Those negatively affected would grumble, "Instead of doing these stupid things, why can't these people just be grateful for their daily bread?"

State media reports on such events were generally vague, contradictory, and unpersuasive. Suspicions, guesses, and rumors spread rapidly. Government propaganda insisted that all such violent events were carried out by separatists and terrorists who aimed to split Xinjiang from China and establish an independent East Turkestan. The government refused to acknowledge any potential causes for the violence in its own policies and in Uyghurs' own lives.

Among Uyghurs, though, all manner of accounts circulated about the origins of these attacks. For the most part, these accounts portrayed the authors of the attacks as having been victims of state injustice, bent on revenge. There were even those who believed that the government itself planned and carried out the violent incidents to provide a pretext for further repression, and to break Uyghurs' will to resist.

In addition to punishing the individuals involved in each violent incident, it was the government's practice to harshly punish people who had nothing to do with the incident but who were in some way related to the perpetrators: their relatives and acquaintances, people who had once shared a meal with them, people who had once had them over as houseguests. Such people were accused of having "taken terrorists under their wing."

Like many other Uyghur intellectuals, I was quite interested to know how these incidents were reported in foreign media and what sort of reaction they elicited abroad. Following the 2009 violence in Urumchi, the internet was shut down in the Uyghur region for nearly a year. Even after it reopened, numerous foreign websites—especially news websites—were blocked; accessing them was considered a serious crime. Despite this, we furtively used VPNs to circumvent the state's notorious Great Firewall and peruse various international news websites. We had so little access to information about our own homeland and what was happening around us that we were willing to take that risk.

Now, as state surveillance and control grew still tighter following Ilham Tohti's arrest and the string of violent incidents, there remained little choice but to delete our VPNs and forgo international websites entirely. Without the opportunity to use the global internet, it seemed that listening to foreign news with a shortwave radio might be my only option.

That summer vacation, our family went to Kashgar. We visited my parents and spent time with old friends. The husband of one of Marhaba's college classmates sold electric appliances at a shopping mall in Kashgar. I decided to buy a shortwave radio from him; I figured he could recommend a good one.

When I walked into his store, he was busily packing the radios displayed on his shelves into their boxes and stacking the boxes in large cartons. After we greeted each other, I asked what he was doing. "The police station called," he said bitterly. "We're to gather up all the radios in the store. From now on we're not allowed to sell radios."

It seemed the list of banned items had grown still longer. A few years earlier, the government had banned matches. Rumor had it that the state was trying to prevent separatists from fashioning explosives out of the sulfur in match heads.

That was the end of my plan to purchase a radio. A few days later, I heard that police had begun confiscating radios from people's homes, first in the villages, then in the cities.

It seems the radio era is coming to an end, I said to myself.

I was born at the very end of the 1960s in a poor, unattractive little settlement on the northwestern edge of the Taklamakan Desert. This settlement was a production brigade in the Peyzawat Land Reclamation Sector, which belonged to the third division of the Xinjiang Production and Construction Corps. The production brigades in the sector were situated several kilometers from one another; traveling between brigades meant a trip down dirt roads through the desert. Residents lived in simple, identical mud-brick homes provided by the government. When there was tilling and harvesting to be done, members of the brigade worked collectively in the wide fields surrounding the settlement. These fields were newly reclaimed land. Carrying their mattocks on their shoulders, brigade members would walk together to the fields. Salaries were equal. Food—primarily corn flour—was provided according to quota. Meat, oil, rice, vegetables, fruit, and wheat flour were precious commodities. Sometimes we would go months without seeing sugar.

Where we lived, the most prized possessions were bicycles, wrist-watches, and radios. A radio was the most important means of under-standing the outside world and the leading source of entertainment. Each radio had chrome casing and a belt to hang around your neck. Men would strap on their wristwatches, seat their wives on the backs of their bicycles, and turn up the volume on the radios hanging around their necks as they rode to and from the bazaar. These were their happiest moments. My mother and father would ride like that to the bazaar, and in the evening would bring me back a round *girde* roll made from real wheat flour—not that coarse corn flour we always ate—and four or five candies. I would be the happiest kid in the world.

My father's beloved radio usually hung from a post in our house. No one was allowed to touch it. We listened to the state's propaganda news items, the weather reports that were always wrong, and the songs praising the party. My mom would hum along to the songs as she did housework.

The neighborhood kids would take apart old broken radios. We looked with fascination at the parts, unable to imagine how sound could emerge from them. It was the magnet behind the speaker that interested us most. We liked to remove the magnet and use it to find nails we buried under the sand. The magnet's iron-pulling magic amazed us.

One morning, there was a big commotion in the broad courtyard in front of our house. When I ran outside, I saw a policeman in his black-brimmed white cap, white jacket, and blue pants alongside two People's Militia members in civilian clothing with red armbands and guns. They were marching along a man with his hands tied behind his back and a tall paper hat on his head. From the looks of it, they had paraded this man on foot all the way from another production brigade. The policeman was saying something to the people gathered around them. My mom put down her laundry and joined me out in the courtyard. The two of us approached the crowd. I wasn't able to push through, though, and couldn't tell what was happening. After a little while the crowd began to disperse. We went home, too.

"What happened to that man?" I asked my mom.

"He listened to the Soviet revisionists' radio station," she replied sadly.

I grew still more interested. "How did he manage to listen to it?"

"During collective labor he excused himself to use the bathroom, hid behind a tamarisk bush, and took out the radio he had tucked away in his clothes. While he was listening to dirty songs from Tashkent, someone found him and told the brigade leader." Her tone was solemn.

"What will they do with him now?" I asked.

My mom lowered her voice a little. "It's been a month since they caught him. For the last five days they've been parading him around, brigade by brigade. Looks like they'll sentence him soon." She looked nervously toward the open door.

"What's a dirty song?"

My mother continued washing the laundry. "A dirty song is a bad song."

"What kind of bad song?" I asked, undeterred.

"You're still little," sighed my mom. "Don't worry about it."

After a little while, I stepped outside to take a look. It was noon on a summer day, and the weather was scorching. The courtyard was empty, aside from the poor man in the paper hat sitting in the center. The policeman and the two people's soldiers must have left to eat lunch at the brigade leader's house.

I suddenly realized how thirsty I was. Stepping back inside, I filled a mug with water from the bucket in the corner and drank it in one go. Then it occurred to me how thirsty that man must be. "Should I bring him some water?" I asked my mother. Without getting up from her laundry, my mom craned her head to glance outside. "OK."

I took a full mug of water and walked up to the man. He was sitting with his head hanging down and didn't even sense that I had approached him. I held the mug up, directly in front of his eyes; startled, he raised his head and looked at me. The man was older than my father. His pallid face was smeared with black. His beard was overgrown, his lips chapped. The tall pointy hat on his head, made from newspaper, would make anyone look ridiculous. His hands were tied behind him, so I held the mug to his lips. He drank the water just as I had, in a single gulp. He looked at me and smiled. I turned and ran back home.

For years I couldn't stop wondering what a dirty song was. Later I learned that the "dirty songs" the man had listened to were in fact Uyghur folk songs broadcast on Tashkent radio. Many Uyghur folk songs center on romantic love, and in those years when humanity was denied and each person was a cog in the giant revolutionary machine, such songs were banned as "dirty songs." Many other people in that period were punished for "listening to reactionary propaganda on enemy radio." In the Uyghur region, "enemy radio" largely referred to radio stations in the Soviet Union's Central Asian republics.

The situation improved considerably in the early 1980s. Listening to foreign radio ceased to be considered a crime, and Uyghur folk songs previously considered "dirty songs" were played freely on the Uyghur region's radio stations. But the Chinese government's information blockade did not slacken altogether. Even after film, television, and cassette recordings began to replace the radio in people's lives, many still used shortwave radios to access otherwise restricted information from foreign radio programs.

Concerned by this, the Chinese government began taking measures to block the reception of foreign radio signals. In particular, following the 2009 Urumchi incident, the government increased funding for radio jamming equipment to prevent "the infiltration of enemy forces and ethnic splittist forces from abroad." Many people, however, refused to give up listening to foreign radio. In early 2010, a friend of mine from Hotan told me proudly how his younger brother could calibrate a radio such that it would only receive Radio Free Asia's Uyghur-language service, and with a very clear signal. His younger brother had studied electrical engineering in college. I heard that he adjusted the shortwave radios of quite a few people in this way.

Now, by prohibiting the sale of shortwave radios and confiscating them from Uyghurs who already owned them, the government was seeking to completely cut off access to information from abroad. Unable to visit foreign websites or listen to radio from other countries, we suddenly found ourselves living like frogs at the bottom of a well.

My Hubris

I n autumn 2015, while I was on site filming the television series *Kashgar Story*, a weeklong shoot was planned in Moosh, a village thirty-five kilometers west of Kashgar City. The village had a number of locations that fit our needs for various scenes. One morning at daybreak, along with several members of our film crew, I drove out to Moosh to select shooting locations. We sped past the white poplars lining the road on both sides, their yellow leaves shining in the morning sun.

The village of Moosh held special importance for me. Several kilometers from the village center, on a gravelly plain along the road, stood the Kashgar Reeducation Through Labor Camp. For a year and a half, I had been a prisoner there. Now, for the first time since my release, I had returned.

My colleagues continued their lively conversation as we drove, but I was lost in thought as memories of that time flooded back.

The reeducation camp was a kilometer or two to the left of the road.

From the road I could see the copse of trees where the complex stood: it was still there. I looked at the gravelly plain where we had once performed hard labor, but today I saw no prisoners working there. I had heard that the camp now housed "frightening" prisoners; it had apparently been made into a secret prison. Given that the prisoners were referred to only as "frightening," with the nature of their crimes undisclosed, I concluded that they must be political prisoners sentenced to lengthy terms.

I was still ruminating when one of my colleagues pointed to an enormous, newly built complex on the right side of the road. "That's the women's prison," he said with animation. The high walls of the complex were topped with barbed wire and fitted with surveillance cameras. We passed by the massive black gate, where a sign written in Chinese identified the facility as Kashgar Women's Prison. Behind the gate were row after row of gray buildings. It was silent and cold, with not a soul in sight. I knew prisons, and I shuddered to think of what must happen in those gray buildings.

That morning we found two of the locations we needed for filming, a sheep farm and a stony field in the foothills. We needed to find a farmer's house as well, and after lunch we went in search of one. The Uyghur village head, who was accompanying us, listened to our requirements. He led us over to a house belonging to the imam of the neighborhood mosque. Looking over the house, it became clear that it didn't meet our needs, and we prepared to take our leave. The imam, though, felt honored by this visit from the village head, and insisted that we all stay for tea. We could hardly refuse, so we took a seat.

We chatted over medicine tea, blowing on our cups to cool the piping hot liquid. In Uyghur custom, a meal was usually prepared for guests; but our host, knowing we wouldn't be staying long, raced over to the bazaar on his motorcycle and brought back several dozen meat-filled *samsa*. He laid the succulent dumplings, still warm from the oven, on a tablecloth.

Just as we began eating, we suddenly heard the Chinese song "Little Apple" coming from somewhere. The imam pulled his phone out of his pocket. The song was his ringtone: he had a call. He stepped outside to talk.

After the 2009 Urumchi incident, Wang Lequan, the party official who had ruled Xinjiang for fifteen years, was transferred away from his post, and Zhang Chunxian became party secretary of the Uyghur region. Not long after Zhang arrived, the regional government arranged for the song "Little Apple" to be played ceaselessly in all of the region's public spaces, schools, and even private stores and restaurants. It became a plague. People called the tune "Zhang's favorite song." Zhang must have heard the song somewhere and mentioned to his underlings that he liked it; perhaps they were trying to curry favor with him by blanketing the entire region with the song.

Recently, the government had even arranged for Islamic clerics to dance along to "Little Apple." The state organized public disco contests for the clerics and broadcast them widely on television. Pity and anger welled up in us when we saw these respected, dignified religious leaders, who generally refrained from entertainment, forced to dance disco onstage. For their part, they gritted their teeth and tried not to acknowledge how ridiculous and pathetic their situation was. Forcing these ab-surdities on our clergy was a flagrant insult to them and to our faith, but there was nothing we could do about it.

The imam returned from his phone call and took a seat. "Are you also dancing to 'Little Apple'?" I asked him. The imam looked a bit taken aback at the unexpected question, but he kept his composure. "We are," he replied. "No harm comes of it, and it's good exercise." From the way he said it, it was clear he did not appreciate the question and was doing his best to avoid further discussion. With the village head present, what else could he have said? I immediately regretted asking.

I was reminded of something I had witnessed four years earlier. In autumn 2011, at the invitation of the local culture bureau, I had traveled to Kucha County to produce a number of music videos for Kucha folk songs. For one of the videos, we needed fifty or sixty extras; we would hire them from among the local farmers. Along with the head of the county culture bureau, I went to meet with the village head, also a Uy-ghur, to explain what we needed. The shoot was to be held the following day, October 1, which happened to be National Day in China.

The village head listened to our request. "Tomorrow they'll be rais-ing the flag at all Friday mosques. We can make arrangements with the farmers after the ceremony."

I was shocked. "What are you saying?" I muttered aloud to myself. "Now they're raising the flag at mosques?"

The village head and the two village cadres sat there in silence. Their deep distress was palpable, and I knew their hands were tied.

Raising the Chinese flag at Uyghur houses of worship was unheard of. Even during the Cultural Revolution, nothing of the kind had happened. Forcing us to fly this flag at our holiest sites was yet another reminder that we had been colonized. I heard that the government was also forcing Tibetans to raise the Chinese flag at their temples.

Now, four years after the Chinese flag was raised at Uyghur mosques, Uyghur religious leaders were being forced to dance disco for public display.

The day after we went to scout filming locations in Moosh, I was busy shooting a scene when my phone rang. It was the head of the company financing the series. After inquiring how the filming was progressing, the financier's tone grew serious.

"I have something urgent I need to tell you. From now on, we won't be using the words *assalamu alaikum* and *wa alaikum assalam* ['Peace be upon you,' 'And upon you, peace'] in the series. The television station received a directive from the Autonomous Region Party Committee Propaganda Department. Just now I got a call from the head of the TV station."

Since the series would be broadcast on Xinjiang Television Station, we had no choice but to accept the station's frequent political oversight. As required by regulation, once our screenplay was completed it was translated into Chinese and submitted to a special government inspection committee. When the committee opined that our screenplay failed to emphasize the party's benevolence toward Uyghurs, we were forced to add such content in a number of places. The committee then noted that there were no Han characters in the screenplay; they told us to add some. Although the series was entirely concerned with Uyghur life, there was nothing for us to do but find a way to add a couple of Han characters. Following months of revision, with great difficulty we got the thirty-part series approved. After filming was completed, the series would need to pass through a further round of political inspection.

Aside from this, we needed to prepare Chinese subtitles for the entire Uyghur-language series. I had never heard of a Han person watching a Uyghur television program; perhaps Han who know Uyghur flip through those channels occasionally. Han in Xinjiang rarely watch even the Chinese-language Xinjiang TV channels, preferring the channels produced by their own home provinces in inner China. This business of creating Chinese subtitles for Uyghur programs was in fact just another way to monitor Uyghurs.

Like colonists in European empires, Han settlers looked down on the native peoples of the Uyghur region. The great majority of them thought the Uyghur language was not worth learning. Yet because they did not know the language, Uyghur society seemed foreign and inscrutable to these Han residents of the region, which gave them a constant sense of unease. Now Uyghur television programs, which had already passed through layer after layer of government inspection, were available with their subtitles for the viewing and inspection of any Han citizen at any time they chose.

To inspect the Chinese subtitles for these programs, an experienced editor called Alim was called out of retirement. Given that the subtitles were a "political responsibility," filmmakers were exceedingly careful and diligent in preparing them, and they were generally free of error.

Alim, however, was preoccupied with the most minute matters of grammar. In particular, he carefully scrutinized the grammatical particles *de*, *di*, and *de*, which in Chinese sound similar but have different grammatical roles. Filmmakers called him "Alim Particle."

While I was irritated by the *assalamu alaikum* directive, I wasn't surprised. Recent years had taught us to expect this kind of absurdity.

"What are we supposed to say instead?" I asked.

"They didn't tell us. I imagine we can say 'Are you doing well?,' 'How have you been?,' and so on."

"Is there a written directive from the Propaganda Department?"

The financier hesitated, then spoke decisively. "Don't worry about that. All you have to do is follow this directive while shooting the rest of the series."

"Hold on a minute," I said. "Let me get this clear. Is there or isn't there a written directive? Can you tell me that?"

"I'm told it was a verbal directive. The words *assalamu alaikum* and *wa alaikum assalam* are not to be used in radio, film, television, or publishing." He said all this nonchalantly, as if relating something completely ordinary.

"We've already filmed more than half of the thirty episodes," I said with annoyance. "We used these words in all of them, just as the script called for and just as Uyghurs do in everyday life when greeting each other. How does it make any sense at this point to tell us not to use them?"

"I understand that, but what can we do?" The financier took a more menacing tone. "If this results in the serial being barred from broadcast, who will take responsibility for my millions of yuan in losses?"

"Look," I explained to him, "TV dramas are a representation of life, they narrate stories. If the Propaganda Department wants to ban these words, first let them issue a policy or a directive prohibiting the use of these words in Uyghur daily life. Then we can stop using the words in TV and film as well."

All this was too much for him to accept. He moved on to straightforward threats. "I've relayed the directive to you. If you ignore it, you will be responsible for the consequences."

"That's fine," I replied. "I'll keep shooting according to script. If we really do have to change it, let's finish filming first and then fix all the episodes at once after we return to Urumchi. We can simply dub over those parts of the actors' lines."

He seemed to find this acceptable. His tone softened a bit. "OK. Really, though, if we don't handle this well, we will all be in hot water."

I continued filming according to script. Ten or so days later, an actor arrived from Urumchi to film a part in the series. When the two of us met to discuss his role, he told me that the *assalamu alaikum* directive had been rescinded.

Not long after, I heard how all of this had come about. A theater exhibition for the whole autonomous region had been held in Urumchi, with troupes from every district performing dramas and operas. A Han deputy chief of the regional Propaganda Department had taken part in reviewing the performances. While watching a play performed by the Ili Song, Dance & Theater Troupe, this deputy chief seems to have been disconcerted by the greetings *assalamu alaikum* and *wa alaikum assalam*. Turning to the Uyghur cadre beside him, he asked the meaning of these phrases. The cadre explained in Chinese that it was the same as the common Uyghur greeting *yaxshimusiz*, "Are you doing well?" But the deputy chief barked at the cadre that he knew the word *yaxshimusiz*. The Uyghur cadre was reduced to silence, and the deputy chief ordered him to ascertain immediately the meaning of *assalamu alaikum*.

The cadre immediately called an Islamic scholar who worked for the government and asked him the meaning of the phrase. The scholar told the cadre it was an Arabic phrase, taught by Muhammad to his disciples. Its full form was *assalamu alaikum wa rahmatullahi wa barakatuh*, meaning "May God's peace, mercy, and blessings be upon you." The full form of the reply to this greeting was *wa alaikum assalam wa rahmatullahi wa barakatuh*, which means "May God's peace, mercy, and blessings be upon you as well." The scholar explained that people typically used the abbreviated versions *assalamu alaikum* and *wa alaikum assalam*, meaning "May peace be upon you."

On learning that these were religious greetings, the deputy chief was enraged. He issued an oral directive strictly prohibiting the use of the phrases *assalamu alaikum* and *wa alaikum assalam* in any media, including radio, film, television, newspapers, and journals.

Before long, however, the directive was voided for some reason. I figured it must have been the force of public reaction. It's not so easy to restrict the customs and beliefs that a people have cherished for a thousand years, I thought to myself with some hubris.

One day at lunchtime, while we were in the final stages of filming *Kashgar Story*, a few lads from the lighting crew were sitting next to me, looking at a phone held by one of them. "Is that the list we were just talking about?" the others asked eagerly. "Give it here, let's take a look."

"Yeah," replied the phone's owner. "It's the list of banned names. Bin Laden, Saddam, Hussein, Arafat . . ."

One of the others interrupted. "But there aren't any Uyghurs named Bin Laden or Saddam, are there?"

"Maybe someone named their children that," cut in another. "You know our people love the latest fad!"

"I've literally never heard of it," said the young man who had spoken previously.

By now, the phone's owner had finished reading the list. I asked him to send it to me, which he did without delay. Titled "List of Prohibited Names," the document had been issued by a neighborhood government office and contained fifteen male names alongside seven female names, all arranged neatly in a little chart. Some of the names, such as Hussain, Saifuddin, Aisha, and Fatimah, have been widely used by Uyghurs for centuries. Other names—Arafat, Munisa, and others—had become fashionable in the 1990s. Names like Saddam and Guldullah, also on the list, were quite rare among Uyghurs. I had never heard of a Uyghur naming their child Bin Laden.

Although the document did not explain why these names had been forbidden, one could see at a glance that the names had been selected as excessively "ethnic" or "religious," and that they had been banned as a measure against purported religious extremism. This was an ill omen. A name is a human's most personal possession; if he cannot hold on to his own name, what hope does he have of keeping anything else?

A year and a half later, the regional government circulated another list of prohibited Uyghur names. The two-page list included twenty-nine male and female names. In addition to a number of extremely common names with religious origins—Muhammad, Haji, Imam, Islam, and others—the list also outlawed names with an ethnic character like Turkzat and Turkinaz.

I had a friend named Memet who worked as an editor at a literary journal. In publications, he had been in the habit of using his name's original Arabic form, Muhammad. Once the name Muhammad had been banned, however, he went back to writing his name "Memet." In reality, "Memet" and "Muhammad" are merely the Uyghur and Arabic pronunciations of the same name. Yet this distinction now determined whether or not one was a religious extremist. Anyone considered an extremist by the government would know no end to their troubles.

Another well-known writer used the pen name "Turan." This word, which refers to ancient Central Asia and the collective homeland of the Turkic peoples, was now forbidden as "promoting pan-Turkist ideas." The writer swiftly abandoned his pen name.

Bans were even issued against various place names. My parents are from Kashgar's Peyzawat County, and whenever they took me as a kid to see family there, our relatives would take us to eat at the Peach Village bazaar. One of the neighborhoods in Peach Village was called Islam Boat, a rather unusual name that lodged in my memory. In spring 2017, I heard from relatives in Peyzawat that this neighborhood's name had been changed simply to Boat. Not far away, in Red Village, a neighborhood named Halal had its name changed to Orchard. I learned of similar name changes in other towns: in Hotan's Lop County, for example, Islam'awat became simply Awat.

Around that time, I went to take care of some business at a lawyer's office. In the waiting room, I picked up a July 21 copy of the *Xinjiang Gazette* from the coffee table. Flipping through the newspaper, a series of announcements about name changes caught my eye.

"My son's birth name was Arafat Ablikim (ID number XXX)," read a typical item. "From now on, he will be known as Bekhtiyar Ablikim." This announcement was signed by Ablikim Ghopur of so-and-so neighborhood in so-and-so village, Yéngisar County.

Another person announced that they had changed their daughter Muslima's name to Marhaba; another that their daughter Nur'islam was now Pezilet; another that he had changed his own name from Ababekri (Abu Bakr) to Esqer.

Typically, if ID cards or other important credentials were lost, the government departments charged with replacing them would require those who had lost their documents to place an ad in a regional-level newspaper, reporting the loss and declaring that the credentials were henceforth null and void. Needless to say, it was fairly expensive to place such announcements in a newspaper, but given the importance of ID documents, people were willing to shoulder the cost. Now people were paying to announce in the newspapers that they had given up their own names in accordance with the state's restrictions.

By the end of the year, people had been obliged to drop the word "Allah" and use "my lord" instead. For example, anyone wanting to use the common Uyghur farewell pleasantry "I entrust you to God" had to use the awkward formulation "I entrust you to my lord" instead. If one wanted to convey mourning and blessings on social media for a famous person who had passed away, the usual phrase "May they rest in heaven" could not be used; the best people could manage was "May their resting place be beautiful." No Uyghur dared utter the greetings *assalamu alaikum* and *wa alaikum assalam*.

By then, I knew that my hubris had come too soon.

The Women's Prison

Autumn was a jumble of colors

staining our clothes as we walked the road

In the clay-bedded stream beside us

God's cold water was flowing

In the water swirled leaves with holes

We passed a wide bare enclosure

A red light on the gate was shining like Satan

Qasimjan pointed

—That's the women's prison

His friend Rozakhun grinned

—I wouldn't mind being locked in a cell full of women

The body of the land was in pieces

The roads were stitching them together

Cold air was leading its kin

down from the mountain

A sudden shiver went through me

THREE

Uninvited Guests

I arrived half an hour early to the private dining room. We had reserved the restaurant's largest room a week earlier. Including myself, sixteen people—writers, translators, musicians—had signed up to attend our first poets' gathering of 2016.

When I walked into the room, the poet-bookseller Eli was joking around with the translator-shopkeeper Almas.

"I see you brought two watermelons, Master Almas. Are you feeling summery even in the dead of winter?" Eli pointed to the fruit Almas had brought for our event.

"That's right," Almas shot back. "The benevolence of the party has warmed my heart." We all laughed.

The other guests began to arrive one by one. We all knew each other and we greeted each other warmly, with jokes and laughter and easy conversation. After more or less everyone had already arrived, one poet we all knew appeared with two strangers, introducing them as poets who had heard about today's event and wanted to join. From everyone's expressions, it was clear no one else knew the pair. It seemed no one had even run across their names in any journals. The two unknown poets seemed a bit embarrassed.

In the current climate, at group events like this, Uyghurs were increasingly wary of unfamiliar guests, fearing that they might be government informers. In Uyghur society, though, poets and writers are a tight-knit group, supporting each other and seeking out each other's company. Getting to know new writers is a regular occurrence. After a moment of awkwardness and doubt, we all snapped out of it and continued our conversations.

A year earlier, I had gotten the idea of organizing occasional events for Uyghur poets. Although the government's escalating stability-preservation measures were constricting ever further Uyghurs' ability to gather, it was worth taking advantage of what space remained. Spending time together and exchanging ideas was good for poets' creativity.

The novelist Perhat Tursun and I planned the first event. In my We-Chat friend circle, I posted a simple announcement that we would be holding a poets' gathering in Urumchi at the end of May, and that those interested in attending should contact me. Within days, more than twenty people had signed up. Most were poets and translators based in Urumchi, but a few people would be coming from Ghulja, Turpan, and Korla. A couple of people even planned to make the fifteen-hundred-kilometer journey from southern locales like Kashgar and Hotan specifically for this event.

In Dawan, an Urumchi neighborhood with a large Uyghur population, there was a teahouse I knew that seemed perfect. It served both Uyghur and Western food. We decided that a meal would be provided at the event, with Urumchi participants paying the tab, given that we were the hosts. In the current climate, if we held an event without a meal, we might draw the attention of the neighborhood committee cadres prowling the streets. They would worry that our poetry event might be an antigovernment gathering, and immediately report us to the police. If the cops came, even if we avoided a serious incident, it would certainly mean trouble. If we held the event over a meal, we could simply say we were having a lunch party and hopefully avoid any difficulties.

At the event, four of us gave short talks on poetry criticism, while the rest recited some of their own poems. The conversation over lunch was lively. We all left feeling inspired, and agreeing that we should keep having events like this.

A couple of months later, we held the second poets' meetup in the scenic Southern Mountains near Urumchi. More than twenty of us sat around an enormous tablecloth in a yurt we rented from some Kazakh herders. After the poems and literary discussions, we feasted on lamb soup, big plate chicken, salty milk tea, tart *süzme* cottage cheese, and naan flatbread. In the cool mountain air, some strong black tea hit the spot.

Today was our third poets' gathering. As we sat around chatting before the event began, Perhat Tursun walked into the private dining room. After greeting everyone, he came over to me. I could sense how anxious and unnerved he was. I shot him a questioning glance, and he leaned discreetly over to whisper in my ear.

"We've got a problem. We shouldn't have met up today," he said with agitation. "When I came in just now, there was a police car in front of the gate. The two pricks sitting in the car were staring at me."

"Don't get paranoid." There was a note of ridicule in my voice. Perhat had a tendency to worry unnecessarily. "They might have come here to eat and drink like the rest of us."

Perhat dropped the issue, but he remained on edge.

Although I thought Perhat's suspicions were unfounded, some defensive measures seemed prudent in case he was right. Calling Almas over, I asked him to add a couple of bottles of *baijiu* liquor to the food we had already ordered. "Are you getting thirsty?" he joked. We generally didn't serve alcohol at these events, and Almas knew I'm not much of a drinker. But if Perhat was right and the police had come to investigate, they would be less suspicious if a bottle of alcohol on the table confirmed we weren't devout Muslims. The government preferred Uyghurs who spent their time on parties and entertainment.

In the mid-1990s, in an effort to combat a rising tide of alcoholism, gambling, and heroin use, Uyghurs in Ghulja revitalized the traditional practice of *meshrep*. In addition to singing, dancing, and other entertainment, people at *meshrep* ridiculed bad habits by meting out comedic punishments; they talked of heaven and hell and built up pressure in society for young people to take the right path. The local government, however, banned *meshrep*, claiming that it encouraged religious extremism.

Not to be deterred, Uyghur youth organized soccer teams in an effort to promote healthy living through sports. Once again, though, the government forbade them to continue and violently suppressed their protests.

At our poets' gathering this evening, we hoped the two bottles of alcohol on the table might prove a magical artifact, transforming us into the kind of Uyghurs the government desired, the kind who had their fun and didn't make trouble.

As we began eating, the waitress came in with a pot of tea. "*Aka*, which one of you is the host?" She was looking in my direction, having sensed that I was the main organizer of the event.

"Is something the matter?"

"Two guests outside are asking for you," she replied a bit uncertainly.

"Tell them to come in," I said without further thought.

She looked toward the door. "They're asking for the host to come out."

Only then did I realize that Perhat's suspicions had been correct. By that point we all understood it was the police who waited outside the door. The room fell silent.

"I'll go." The poet who spoke up was a charming fellow who had lived in Beijing for many years. He was a musician and singer as well. We always described him as someone who had boiled in many pots. He was the kind of guy who could handle a situation like this.

"OK. Go check it out," I said.

He left the room. I turned to a poet who I knew was fond of drinking, and gestured for him to open the *baijiu* bottle and start pouring.

poets' works had been published without issue, and indeed had been the subject of official state commemorations. It seemed things were now taking a different turn.

The police officers' unexpected visit to our poetry gathering reminded me of an incident in Toqsun a year earlier. A local high school had hosted a conference on language pedagogy attended by more than fifty Uyghur schoolteachers. After the conference concluded, the participants gathered for a picnic in a nearby park. As is the custom, several senior teachers were invited to speak. One of them, a seasoned Chinese-language instructor who had been named a model educator at the national level, complained briefly in his remarks about the Uyghur language's increasing marginalization in the education system. Several days later, every teacher who attended the picnic was detained for questioning, with nearly all of them ultimately punished. That senior teacher was sentenced to seven years.

Of course, given the severity of the political climate, we were all very careful. Nothing would be said at the poets' event that might upset the government's delicate nerves. Although I mentioned Alishir Nava'i and Abdukhaliq Uyghur in the announcement, there was nothing related to them in the event's program. We had simply felt that timing the event to coincide with their birthdays was a way to commemorate them.

Now it was my turn to speak. I began reading my recent poem "Road."

> Let there be a man who lived through the winter
>
> Let him fill his inner pocket with rain

and find a farmer

sowing his fields with wind seeds

and let him say to the farmer: "Here I am"

On his return let him seek cotton at seven houses

and show it to me pressed between his fingers . . .

Just as I finished reciting the first stanza, the waitress walked back into the room. I trailed off. The waitress's discomfort was evident, but she spoke courteously. "I'm sorry, but the police are requesting all of your ID cards so that they can record them."

These days, no Uyghur would leave home without their ID card. We all dug our IDs out of our pockets. With considerable professionalism, the waitress collected the cards on a tray and left the room.

The mood had been lost. Even so, I forged ahead, reading my poem again from the beginning. Before long, the waitress returned with our ID cards.

The event continued according to schedule. Those who had prepared talks gave their talks, those with poems read their poems. We got to know those two unfamiliar poets and realized that our worries about them had been unnecessary. But a gloomy mood had settled over the event.

"Have the officers left?" I asked the waitress as she poured my tea.

"Not yet. They're eating and having a few drinks in the next room over."

"How many of them are there?"

"Seven or eight."

This startled us. We had thought only a couple of cops were keeping tabs on our party. To give both ourselves and the officers a little peace of mind, our poet friend who had "boiled in many pots" walked over to the cops' room and joined them for a little while, drinking, joking, and performing a few songs.

The event ended. We posed for a few group photos and took our leave of one another.

Perhat and I were the last to leave, after taking care of the check. As we walked out of the restaurant's courtyard, Perhat spoke in a low, troubled voice. "Tahir, let's not hold events like this anymore."

"I know," I replied with bitter reluctance. "We probably shouldn't."

After that, we walked without saying a word. The cold February wind stung our faces as it whistled around the dark corners.

FOUR

Eli the Bookseller

Sitting in front of my office computer, I felt a headache coming on. I decided to drop by Eli's bookstore.

The 2016 winter had arrived early in Urumchi. It snowed heavily in the beginning of November, and the temperature fell quickly. The roads were coated by a thin layer of ice, and pedestrians chose their steps carefully to avoid slipping.

I walked east down Unity Road, toward the old porcelain factory. Eli's one-room bookstore was right along this road, and I often dropped by to chat. Other friends and acquaintances would also come by, and the conversation was invariably lively.

Eli was a poet, and had been an active participant in all three of our poets' gatherings. Born and raised in a village in the south, he had graduated from Xinjiang University in the early 2000s with a degree in Uyghur literature, after which he remained in Urumchi. He worked a few different jobs, never staying at one for long. When he was unemployed, he was known to assist various researchers with their writing; he made ends meet with the modest remuneration they provided.

Due to his long hair, his fondness for drink, and his carefree, absent-minded nature, Eli's friends nicknamed him "the mystic." Despite his widowed mother's hopes, Eli remained a bachelor as he neared his fortieth birthday.

Finally, with the financial assistance of a group of friends, Eli had opened this bookstore a couple of years before. To assist, I had donated a dozen copies of my book *Trends in Western Modernist Literature*. This was a volume Eli knew well.

The book, the first to systematically introduce Western modernist literature in Uyghur, had been published in January 2000. Back then, on a frigid Urumchi day, I had gone with a friend to a small print shop outside the city, where we loaded three thousand copies of the book into a van. It took us a full day to transfer them all to my friend's clammy basement. I had never realized how heavy books could be.

As I was trying to figure out how to distribute the volumes, Eli and another student from Xinjiang University's literature department came to see me. They asked if I would give a lecture about my book at the university. Although since the 1990s numerous works of Western modernism had been published in Chinese, this book was something new for Uyghurs. According to Eli and his friend, there were a number of students with literary interests who were excited about the book's publication. I accepted their invitation with pleasure.

My lecture had nothing to do with politics. Nonetheless, university regulations required that the students submit a request through their instructors for the administration to authorize my lecture; only after the relevant university offices carried out a political review of the lecture would I be permitted to speak. Handling all this red tape would take quite a while; moreover, a lecture by a poet like me, one who worked outside the state system, was quite unlikely to be approved. Even if approval were forthcoming, the university would send a representative to monitor the lecture. For these reasons, the students simply chose not to inform the university of the lecture, and arranged for it to be held in a classroom that students used for evening study.

As requested, I brought along twenty copies of my book, which I signed and sold before the lecture. I then spoke for about an hour on Western modernist literature. When I finished my talk, Eli was the first to ask a question. After the event had ended, he led several other students in seeing me off to the school gate.

After that, Eli and I saw a fair bit of each other. We discussed literature, Sufi philosophy, Uyghur history, Islam, and various topics of the day in Uyghur society. An orator of considerable skill, Eli knew all manner of stories, and his friends loved to hear him tell them: things never written in history books, things we'd never heard about famous people of the past. He always spoke as convincingly as if he had been there himself. His poems, too, were full of old tales and historical figures.

All of us were pleased when Eli opened the bookstore and finally had a way to earn a regular income. In keeping with his easygoing style, though, he would often sleep till noon and open for business rather late. Some evenings he would forget to lock the store before going home.

Other times he would close the bookstore and disappear without a word for days at a stretch. Since he had no regular cell phone number, getting hold of him was often up to fate.

When I came by his bookstore that day, the diminutive Eli was standing on a chair, arranging volumes on a shelf. The smell of new books filled my nostrils. I liked this smell; it evoked distant memories of my first day of school. Back then, I would flip through each new textbook and breathe in the aroma.

Eli greeted me warmly and invited me to take a seat. While the one-room bookstore was small, it felt rather spacious, since it didn't have that many books.

"I wondered whether you'd be here if I came by," I said.

"I'm here, *aka*," he said, affecting a dignified tone. "Where else would I be?"

"I heard that a week ago you left the bookstore doors wide-open and wandered off again. The doors were open all night. Hopefully nothing was stolen?"

"Come on, *aka*, no one steals books. If I met someone who wanted to steal a book, I'd give it to him for free and treat him to a nice plate of *leghmen* noodles. More to the point, with the situation so tense and police everywhere, with the government having turned citizens into police, what is there for a thief to do? There must be no thieves left," he concluded sagely. I laughed. I liked it when he talked like this.

"How's business?" I asked.

"Not good. If it goes on like this I won't be able to pay the rent. I'll have to close the store."

"Of course business won't be good if you sleep till noon, only open the store in the afternoon, and leave it closed for days at a time," I prodded him.

"That's not the problem, *aka*," he said. "The main issue is that Uyghur publishing is in a shambles thanks to the political situation. Word has gotten around lately that a lot of historical novels have been banned. You know as well as I do that in the Uyghur market, historical novels have always outsold every other genre. But for two months now, publishers have refused to sell us books like *Tracks* and *Motherland*. It seems the rumors are true."

Toward the end of the year, I published my first poetry collection, *The Distance and Other Poems*. I found an inexpensive press and had three thousand copies printed with my own funds. Several months later, after the volumes finally arrived, we held a book signing at Eli's bookstore.

Although I had written poetry since I was sixteen, I'd never been a prolific poet. I lacked commitment to my writing. In addition, my noncomformist poetic style was increasingly distant from the formalist mainstream of Uyghur poetry, which made it progressively more difficult to get published. Perhaps that had dampened my enthusiasm for writing poetry. I wasn't the only poet in that situation.

I hadn't planned to publish a poetry collection at this point. No publisher would pay to put out a volume of my work, which meant I would have to self-publish. But the worsening political climate spurred me into action: if things went on like this, before long it would be even harder to publish Uyghur books. I should publish a collection of my poems while it was still possible. And now that I was finally putting out a collection after so many years of writing, I wanted it to be as good as I could make it—an expensive proposition, needless to say.

The political situation made me exceedingly cautious. As rumors accumulated about "problems" found in various books, fear grew in the hearts of authors like me. After long years writing under state scrutiny, Uyghur authors were generally more vigilant and sensitive than the party's own censors. Even so, it was the state that determined whether a work was problematic, and its standards were growing ever more stringent. If the standards applied to publications happened to shift, and a book previously published was found not to meet the new criteria, it would prove most unfortunate for the author.

Before publishing my collection, then, I sifted carefully through the poems. A number of poems I elected to exclude entirely. In one poem, I omitted the line "You can't imagine a homeland you've never seen," and in another, I changed the line "My mother is no infidel" to "My mother is not without faith."

Once the volume was printed, Eli put a good deal of effort into helping me sell it, as he had with my previous book. A week after the book signing at his store, the two of us decided to see if the Autonomous Region's Xinhua Bookstores would distribute the volume. Xinhua is China's largest state-owned bookseller, with branches in every county. Although

Xinhua was slow and parsimonious with payments for privately published books, it would be a big deal if its chain of bookstores could distribute one or two thousand copies of my collection.

Eli and I headed to Xinhua's minority-language book distribution center in the north of the city. Working in the book trade himself, Eli was familiar with the staff there.

When we arrived, all personnel were in a meeting, so we sat down to wait outside the meeting hall. I could hear Erkin, the center's director, speaking in Chinese. I had known him for a while. In 2001, some time after publishing *Trends in Western Modernist Literature* at my own expense, I had discussed distributing the book with Erkin, then Uyghur-language distribution director for the Autonomous Region's Xinhua Bookstores. Leafing through the copy I had brought, he muttered "a bunch of gobbledygook!" before agreeing to distribute five hundred copies. He was an irritable person with a shrill voice.

It was by his voice that I now recognized him. In dejected tones, he was saying that in thirty years working in book distribution, he had never encountered a situation like the present one.

"He's talking about the banned historical novels," Eli whispered knowingly in my ear.

Following the Urumchi incident in 2009, the regional government had initiated the Looking Back Project. The Propaganda Department organized special groups to go over Uyghur-language books, newspapers, journals, films, television shows, and recordings from the 1980s to the present. These groups were tasked with identifying any materials that contained ethnic separatist themes or religious extremist content.

Two years after the Looking Back Project began, I received an unexpected phone call from Nijat, a photographer I knew who was the fine-arts editor at a well-known Uyghur journal. I'd met Nijat in 2007, when I had directed a documentary in Kashgar on Uyghurs' celebration of Eid al-Adha, part of a series of documentaries commissioned by the government on Uyghur intangible heritage. The film followed a photographer documenting the festival in Kashgar; Nijat was that photographer.

A friend of Nijat's had been assigned to take part in the Looking Back Project. While investigating previously published films, he saw Nijat in the Eid documentary and told him what was going on. Worried for my safety, Nijat had called to make sure everything was all right.

I thanked Nijat and told him that as yet nothing had happened to me. I shuddered, though, to hear that the government was now investigating films that had been commissioned by its own organs and approved for distribution by its own censors.

Several years later, as one result of these investigations, half a dozen Uyghur intellectuals and officials were arrested for editing Uyghur literature textbooks for grades one through eleven. The textbooks had been used in schools for over a decade before the "problem" with them was discovered in 2016. With six people arrested, the problem was apparently quite grave.

Word spread that similar "problems" had been found in nearly all Uyghur historical novels, and that they would soon be banned. The government had even banned a popular historical novel by Seypidin Ezizi, the highest-ranking Uyghur official in the history of the Chinese Communist Party. If the work of such a trusted party veteran could be banned, there was little question what the future held for other Uyghur writers.

"Tahir *aka*, you've been awfully quiet." I emerged from my ruminations as Eli nudged me. "I'm listening to Erkin," I said without missing a beat.

Erkin's high voice quavered from the meeting room. He was exhorting all distribution center employees to ignore rumors, perform their duties well, and trust that all issues would be dealt with appropriately.

After the meeting ended, we found Qadir, the current chief distribution officer, and explained what we had come for. "Poetry books are tough to sell. You'd best take care of it yourself," he replied unceremoniously. "Let's say we take this book from you. If the directors of local Xinhua bookstores don't buy it from us, it'll still gather dust in this storeroom."

There was nothing more to say. We walked wearily out of the distribution center. We had known this was a likely outcome, but at least we'd given it a try.

On the way home, Eli told me how Nationalities Press in Beijing had recently published collections by the prominent poets Adil Tuniyaz and Ghojimuhemmed Muhemmed, only to find that the Xinjiang Uyghur Autonomous Region News and Publishing Office refused to permit their distribution. The head of Nationalities Press's Uyghur division was incensed. "We are a national-level publisher in Beijing. Why won't you let us distribute our books in Xinjiang?"

"In that case, you can distribute your damn books in Beijing," replied the Han director of the News and Publishing Office. "In Xinjiang, whatever we say goes!"

"Han officials couldn't say things like that before," said Eli gloomily. "Things must be pretty bad."

It had generally been rare for the government to ban books that had already been published—first, because any book published had already passed through multiple layers of political inspection, and second, because if the government announced that a book had been banned, the book would immediately become famous, with people finding all manner of ways to get hold of a copy. People who had never heard of the book would suddenly want to read it. Distributed underground, such books appealed to more readers than they ever would have otherwise. As a result, the government was reluctant to declare a ban of any given book, choosing instead to quietly block the sale of the book or to pull it from bookstore shelves.

In the early 1990s, the government banned the poet and historian Turghun Almas's books *The Uyghurs*, *A Brief History of the Huns*, and *Ancient Uyghur Literature*. According to the censors, these three books "promote Uyghur nationalist ideology and advocate ethnic separatism." A public campaign to criticize the books was unfurled across the Uyghur region. Numerous Uyghur intellectuals who had not read the books or even thought of reading them suddenly began lodging sardonic requests with the government. "First provide us copies of the three books. That way we can read them carefully and criticize them more effectively." Everyone knew, of course, that the party would do no such thing, and that it would instead force the populace to read, memorize, and recite prepared criticisms.

Right around then, a friend of mine studying physical education at

Kashgar Teachers College relayed a story to me. One day, a "Great Meeting to Criticize the Three Books and Oppose Ethnic Separatism" was held in the college's open-air summer movie theater. The college's Uyghur administrators took their seats on the stage. The rector began loudly reading out the critical materials distributed by the Autonomous Region Propaganda Department.

By arrangement, as soon as the rector finished reading the materials, a cadre in the college's propaganda office called out, "Destroy the ethnic separatists!" The meeting's program called for students to respond by chanting, "Destroy them!" The students, however, were caught unprepared. They had only seen such slogan chanting in movies. At first, no one repeated the cadre's chant.

"Chant after me!" cried the cadre. "Destroy the ethnic separatists!" This time a few students repeated it after him. But from the section where the physical education students were sitting, one voice could be heard loudly chanting something different. "Moo!"

No one could figure out who exactly had done it. The students began whispering. Some laughed.

Seeing that some students were still not repeating his chant, the cadre raised his voice still further and tried a third time: "Destroy the ethnic separatists!" This time all of the students chanted together. "Moooo!"

Bewildered, the cadre called out, "Long live ethnic solidarity!" This time the students roared still more loudly. "Moooo!"

Observing this spectacle, the rector rose angrily from his seat. "Which of you are mooing?" he yelled. "Get out of your seats!" The students all sat quietly, looking downward. Fuming, the rector glared at the students for a moment, then declared the meeting at an end.

My friend finished his story. "That day we really felt a lot lighter," he told me with some pride. He was silent for a bit, then added sadly, "Sometimes I find myself thinking, perhaps it's better to be a cow than to be a Uyghur."

FIVE

The Red Armband

When I opened the door to Almas's convenience store, there were no customers inside. Almas was sunk in his chair, reading a book. On his left arm was a red armband with "Security" emblazoned on it in yellow Chinese characters. The scene was reminiscent of Red Guards reading Chairman Mao's collected works during the Cultural Revolution.

"Congratulations on the armband!" I teased him.

"Thanks! Does it look good on me?" He smiled impishly.

"This is something new. Looks like the party is giving them out?"

"It's giving them out, but not for free," he said with a grin. "This armband was twenty yuan, that truncheon was thirty yuan, the whistle was ten yuan. That's sixty yuan down the drain."

Propped behind the door was a truncheon about four feet long. Its grip was tapered, and it broadened out toward the end. It looked mass-made. Right next to it, hanging from a nail in the wall, was a yellow plastic whistle fastened to a red ribbon.

"Is every shopkeeper required to buy these?"

"Yeah," he said, scratching his head, "all stores have to keep these items on hand. The neighborhood committee made an announcement. Whenever a store is open, one employee has to sit there wearing this armband. If they catch us not wearing it, they force us to close up shop and they seal the doors. To get the seal removed, we have to go to the neighborhood committee, pay a fine, and write out a guarantee. Have they not made your company do this?"

"No, they haven't had us do that."

"I guess this policy is just aimed at roadside stores." Almas dog-eared the page he was reading and closed his book.

I tried to make him feel better. "They're not leaving us alone, either. In our building, they constantly make us run down to the street to carry out Joint Antiterrorist Maneuvers."

"I haven't been to Eli's bookstore recently." A note of irony crept into Almas's voice. "But I heard he's also sitting in his store with a truncheon propped behind the door, a whistle hanging on the wall, a red band on his arm. I bet the armband looks great with his long hair. I can't wait to see for myself."

"Go a little easier on other people. We all look absurd these days."

Beginning in fall 2016, new "stability preservation" measures were rolled out across the Xinjiang Uyghur Autonomous Region, including in the capital, Urumchi. One of these measures was mobilizing city residents in the private sector into a "United Line of Defense Against Violent Terrorists." This line of defense gathered its forces from the corner stores and office buildings of Urumchi's Uyghur neighborhoods.

Just the other day, I had noticed for the first time that roadside store owners were wearing the armbands. Around noon, Marhaba had asked me to fetch some mutton at the Uyghur butcher shop in front of our apartment complex. When I walked into the shop, I saw the butcher, wearing an armband like Almas's, busily carving up a newly slaughtered lamb that was hanging from a hook. What surprised me even more than his armband was the meter-long chain fixing his knife to a post. The chain was too short to let the butcher move freely, and he was making a clumsy job of the meat carving. I saw that his small meat ax was also chained to the butcher block.

Beginning in October, the neighborhood committees had ordered all restaurants and butcher shops to chain their knives, cleavers, axes, and other blades to fixed objects. Even households now had to register with their IDs in order to purchase knives and cleavers. Word was that in some areas, the customer's ID number had to be carved into the blade upon purchase. The purpose of these measures was clearly to prevent violent terrorists from arming themselves with these blades and attacking others. In the government's view, that butcher was a hidden menace. Now, though, the butcher had strapped on a red armband and joined the front ranks against terrorism.

Almas informed me that his neighborhood committee had divided roadside stores into groups of ten, designating one relatively active shopkeeper as head of each group. The neighborhood committee then required each shopkeeper squad to carry out frequent rapid-response antiterrorist maneuvers. Each maneuver began without warning, when the committee cadre assigned to an area directed the head shopkeeper to blow their whistle. As soon as they heard the whistle, the other shopkeepers in the group would immediately grab their truncheons and gather in the designated place. Following the cadre's orders, sometimes the shopkeepers would march back and forth, searching the neighborhood streets for terrorists. Other times, they would wave their truncheons in the air and practice hitting the terrorists. At first, some were annoyed at this business of pointlessly stomping the streets and punching the air, while others couldn't keep from laughing. But the neighborhood committee cadres repeatedly criticized them and warned them, and gradually they all grew used to it.

"If you're not a group leader, what do you do with your whistle?" I asked.

"If the violent terrorists stir up trouble, each shopkeeper is obligated to immediately blow their whistle. On hearing it, other shopkeepers are to arm themselves with their truncheons and gather in front of the store where the whistle was blown. There we form a line of defense and resist the violent terrorists until the special police arrive."

"If practically everyone is now mobilized to preserve stability, where will the violent terrorists come from?"

"Exactly. This is just another gust of wind," Almas replied knowingly. "After a while it will pass."

While Almas was a dedicated poet with an original style, his greatest success had been in his translation work. He had rendered a number of works by Western philosophers from Chinese into Uyghur; two of these had been published as books. Only those who have translated philosophical texts know how difficult a task it is. Almas's work was much valued in the Uyghur scholarly community.

But he'd always had money troubles. After graduating from Kashgar Teachers College with a degree in Uyghur literature, he had worked as an editor at a Uyghur-language magazine in Urumchi. He had met a beautiful young high school teacher who loved literature, and in summer 2007 they had gotten married.

Almas told me that a couple of years after getting married, he had asked a friend in Norway to send him a letter of invitation so he could apply for a passport and study abroad. The Chinese government placed numerous obstacles in the path of any Uyghur who hoped to obtain a passport. The first of these was requiring them to procure an official invitation letter from another country.

Before Almas had a chance to apply for his passport, he received an unexpected nighttime visit from the very two Uyghur policemen who had questioned me around the same time. Ekber and his assistant Mijit likewise took Almas to the Public Security Bureau's branch office in Tengritagh District, where they interrogated him till daybreak. They were focused in particular on his relationship with that individual in Norway, and on what other contacts he had abroad. Almas obligingly and respectfully answered every question. After Ekber and Mijit had compiled an exhaustive interrogation report, they cautioned Almas to put his passport application on hold for the time being. The next morning they released him, but only after requesting that he stay in frequent touch and that he regularly meet up and chat with them. Eager for the interrogation to end, Almas consented.

For the next two months, Ekber and Mijit repeatedly called Almas and asked to meet. Although Almas didn't have the slightest desire to see them, he was afraid to refuse and felt he had no choice but to go. According to Almas, these meetings did not involve any special discussions. They merely chatted about trivialities over a meal; sometimes, the two cops would insist that they drink together while they ate. Needless to say, Almas picked up the tab for all of these rendezvous.

Almas's salary wasn't high to begin with; his wife had just given birth to a daughter and was not currently employed. Repeatedly treating the policemen to these pointless dinners placed a strain on their finances. His wife complained frequently about it, and Almas himself was fed up with the cops' shameless behavior. Finally, on receiving yet another call from Ekber, Almas spoke heatedly into the phone, just as I had to Mijit. "If I'm guilty of something, arrest me and lock me up. Otherwise, stop bothering me!" After this, Almas stopped taking their calls.

Soon after, a strange thing happened. Almas's boss at the magazine told him that the office was downsizing, and abruptly fired him. Though he had no proof, Almas was certain this was connected to the policemen. Even if he could prove it, though, there was nothing he could do. His family finances grew still more precarious.

Later, Almas's family moved to an apartment complex near ours in Dawan. After a year or so of effort, Almas rented a storefront on the road in front of his complex, and after some renovation opened a convenience store selling various household items. The following year, as the political atmosphere in Urumchi grew harsher, it was this shop that Almas was obliged to fortify as part of the United Line of Defense Against Violent Terrorists.

The campaign Almas had reckoned as a passing wind continued to gather strength. It was growing into a storm, and it would devour everything.

Unity Road

Night fell for the red-blooded,

for the black-blooded as well.

Dawn broke for the forgetful,

for the vengeful as well.

He hurried back from the hot burial,

washing death from his face in the wind,

and then,

from faithful east to fickle west,

from mournful heights to joyous lows,

from familiar edges to the unknown center,

he set off with the step of a man who sinks in.

SIX

Through a Car Window

I had just finished giving my weekly lecture on film directing at Xinjiang Arts Institute when Marhaba called. She told me that our friend Dilber had arrived from Kashgar, and that she was headed to the front gate of the Arts Institute to meet her.

Dilber was the hospitality director of a famous Kashgar hotel. While shooting the television series *Kashgar Story*, our film crew had stayed there for two months. When Marhaba came from Urumchi to visit me for a couple of weeks, she spent time with Dilber at the hotel while we were out filming. Dilber's only son was studying acting at Xinjiang Arts Institute, where I was a visiting professor. We chatted often with Dilber and had a number of meals together; by the time we left Kashgar, we had gotten to know each other well.

Over the phone, Marhaba told me that Dilber's son had been drinking and picking fights in his dorm, and that the institute was threatening to expel him for violating the code of conduct. Dilber had hurried to

Urumchi to plead with school administrators for her son to be allowed to continue his studies.

When I reached the front gate, I saw Dilber standing alone. As I was greeting her, Marhaba arrived. We had barely begun catching up when Dilber burst into tears. Assuming that she was crying for her son, we tried to comfort her. But Dilber was not worried only about her son. She told us what had been happening in Kashgar the past few days.

Mass arrests had begun in Kashgar. The wave of arrests was so immense that existing detention facilities in the city—police station lockups, prisons, holding centers, labor camps, drug-detox stations—were soon overwhelmed. Within days, numerous schools, government offices, and even hospitals had been converted into "study centers," hastily outfitted with iron doors, window bars, and barbed wire. Rumors spread that outside the city, construction was proceeding rapidly on multiple new "study centers," each meant to house tens of thousands. Fear reigned everywhere. People said the Day of Judgment had come.

According to Dilber, the primary targets of these arrests were religiously devout individuals. In addition, no Uyghur who had been abroad, for whatever reason, was to be spared. Only last spring, the Uyghur owner of the hotel where Dilber worked had led a weeklong trip to Dubai for twenty-some outstanding employees, including Dilber. For employees who had served foreign guests for years but had never been abroad themselves, this trip was marvelous and exciting. Now, though, the trip seemed to have brought them catastrophe. Dilber had flown in to Urumchi only yesterday, but this morning she had received a phone call from her local police station in Kashgar, ordering her to return at once. She planned to go back the next morning, after taking care of her son's business. She was clearly terrified that she would be sent to "study" as soon as she returned.

We invited Dilber to lunch, but she had no stomach for it. "Next time," she said forlornly. But no one knew when that next time would come, or if there would be a next time.

Marhaba and I took our leave of Dilber. As I started the car, Marhaba wasted no time in calling my mother in Kashgar to ask how she was doing. My mother confirmed that my relatives in Kashgar were safe, at least for now.

After this, I began paying close attention to the way the mass arrests were unfolding. It was mid-March 2017.

Three days later, as I sat working in my office on a Friday afternoon, I received a phone call from an old friend who had been "reformed" alongside me in the Reeducation Through Labor Camp in Kashgar twenty years earlier. After we exchanged pleasantries, he told me that in Hotan, where he lived, other former inmates from our time in the camp had been arrested one after another over the last several days. His turn was coming soon, he said, and he was worried about me as well. He was relieved to hear that I was still all right. I thanked him and offered some feeble words of comfort. As the conversation came to an end, he spoke in a low voice. "OK, then. I entrust you to God." While his words were a typical adieu in Uyghur, to me they felt like a more final farewell.

A few days passed. I called him, but his phone wasn't on. That week

I called him several times, but his phone remained off. I called three mutual friends in Hotan to ask about him. Their phones were off, too.

Hotan, fifteen hundred kilometers from Urumchi, suddenly seemed even farther away. A strange feeling flashed through me that not a living soul remained there. If things keep on like this, I thought, soon my turn to go "study" will come as well.

It was in 2015 that I had first seen Uyghurs forcibly detained under the euphemism "study."

In late May of that year, I had driven to Turpan to take care of some business. The next day, a poet friend of mine there had invited me to dinner. He asked me to meet him in front of Turpan's new human resources and social services building, to the northeast of the city. I drove over.

Just a few years earlier, this area had been empty, gravelly steppe. Now buildings had been constructed here for a number of city offices and departments, alongside a number of residential complexes.

I found the address my friend had given me. It was a large courtyard flanked by two office buildings. We met in front of the entrance. The gate was bolted shut; in the guardhouse next to it, a Uyghur man in a police uniform sat beside another Uyghur man in civilian dress.

"I'm here to visit my older brother. All I need to do is get him these items." My friend indicated the large plastic sack he was carrying. It looked to contain clothing and personal hygiene items. "This will just take a minute," he told me. "Wait in your car."

My friend spoke to the policeman in the guardhouse and signed himself into the registry book. The cop opened my friend's bag, looked thoroughly through the contents, and put it aside to deliver to his brother. My friend and I headed for the restaurant in my car.

According to my friend, after those offices had been constructed outside town, the old offices in the city center hadn't had a chance to relocate before a "study center" had been opened in the new complex. From four villages in Turpan District, all Uyghurs who had received religious education were to be sent to the center for sixty days of training. Their food and accommodation would be provided inside the courtyard by the government. Except in special circumstances, they would not be permitted outside the center. My friend's older brother was a gentle farmer. Because he had received religious education for a period in his youth, he had recently been sent to the center.

I asked my friend how the authorities determined whether "graduates" of this study center had sufficiently reformed themselves. According to him, each neighborhood's security cadre kept tabs on the graduates and evaluated their degree of reformation. A neighbor of theirs, after completing his "studies" at the center, had traveled to a nearby village on some business. While there, he said his Friday prayers in the village mosque. The cadres responsible for that mosque immediately informed the security cadre in the man's neighborhood that he had entered a mosque where he wasn't registered. The neighbor was taken away to an even stricter "study center" housed in the city police department's detention facility.

These "study centers" in Turpan two years earlier must have been a trial run for the ones now being constructed in Kashgar, Hotan, and other southern areas on a much vaster scale. Perhaps that was why people were optimistic that the detentions would last only a few months. The government's posture, however, gradually made it clear that this campaign would not be so simple.

Although mass arrests had not yet begun in Urumchi, and while some predicted that Urumchi's status as the capital would prevent such things happening there, the internment campaign underway in the south began to affect life in Urumchi as well.

The change was first felt by the countless Uyghurs who had moved over the decades from their hometowns to the capital, where they had worked in various professions and trades, started families, bought houses, and come to consider themselves Urumchi folk. Now they were summoned back to their hometowns by the local police stations where they were still registered. In the Dawan neighborhood, where we lived, the naan bakeries at every crossroads were being boarded up; the fruit sellers' carts were disappearing from the streets; the crowds whose bustle brought the neighborhood to life were dwindling.

Around then, Marhaba observed that our older daughter Aséna, usually quite lively, had been coming home from school in low spirits and heading straight to her room, where she would stay silently for long stretches. Alert to any changes in her daughters, Marhaba knew we needed to act quickly.

When we asked Aséna what was wrong, she told us that over the past week, each day a few of her classmates had quietly disappeared, forced to return with their parents to the towns where they were registered. Several of her good friends were among them. We did our best to comfort Aséna, telling her that her friends might be able to return if the situation improved. Her black eyes, brimming with tears, made it clear she didn't believe us.

One evening a couple of weeks later, toward the end of March, a friend and I decided to unwind at a teahouse in front of my apartment complex. When we arrived, there were no patrons to be seen. The owner was a very friendly young man, and as a frequent customer I had come to know him well. He served us as warmly as he always did, then took a seat at our table to chat. A short while later, a forlorn middle-aged Uyghur man walked into the teahouse and headed straight for a table in the corner. When the owner invited him to join us, the man hesitantly walked over and took a seat. They had met that morning when the man came in for breakfast.

The teahouse proprietor started telling us the man's story. He was from Korla and had lived in Urumchi for over a decade. During that time, he had returned to his hometown to get married and had brought his wife back to Urumchi. They had three children. For the past few years, they had rented a single-story, two-bedroom house in the vicinity, and the man had supported his family with a small welding business in his courtyard. A week ago, he had received a call from the Korla police station where he was registered, ordering him and his family to return to their hometown at once. The welder sent his wife and children ahead of him, and planned to follow them once he had taken care of a few loose ends.

Two days later, though, he was heading to see one of his clients when his ID card set off the alarm on their apartment complex's security scanner. Special police arrived from a nearby People's Convenience Police Post, detained him, and brought him directly to the police station. The officers at the station informed him that his ID had been flagged and that he must immediately contact the officers at the Korla police station where he was registered. When he called the Korla police station, the officer who picked up the phone threatened him in the rudest manner and ordered him to return at once. He begged the officer for more time and managed to get a three-day extension.

The next day—that is, the day before we met him—the neighborhood committee ordered the welder's landlord to evict him. In the freezing weather, he had no choice but to bed down in a cheap hotel nearby.

The welder, who had been sitting quietly, spoke up. "I didn't mind for myself," he said sadly, "but I had quite a few tools and iron materials. My landlord threw them out of the house, too. When I asked him, he wasn't willing to keep them in his courtyard till I returned from Korla. We had gotten along well for so many years, but that meant nothing to him."

It seemed the landlord did not think the man would be returning from Korla.

"What did you do with your materials, then?" my friend asked.

The teahouse owner laughed when he heard the question.

"I couldn't find anywhere to put them," the welder told us. "Looking at it this way and that, I finally thought of the Gülsay Cemetery. I borrowed a wheelbarrow from a junk collector friend of mine, and after night fell I brought my tools and my scrap iron to the graveyard. I lowered them into a pre-dug grave that hadn't been used yet, and then placed the cover back on the grave. Now I just have to hope the grave's owner doesn't die before I return from Korla."

Hearing this, we all laughed, but our hearts were heavy.

"You lived in Urumchi for so many years," I said. "Why didn't you transfer your household registration here?"

"Ah, mister, you city folk don't understand. Villagers like us have a bit of land and our own houses back in our hometowns. The local government will take them away if we transfer our registrations elsewhere. Aside from that, for quite a while now our registration hasn't stopped us from going and living where we liked. We don't know what has happened now."

He would be leaving for Korla in the morning, he told us. He didn't know what awaited him at the police station there.

A few weeks passed, and it was almost May. The Urumchi weather grew warmer.

One Monday morning I drove to the office a bit later than usual. Soon after turning onto Unity Road, I passed by the Bahuliang police station and noticed an unusual commotion in the station courtyard. Slowing my speed, I peered through my car window at the yard. A hundred, perhaps two hundred Uyghurs stood there in silent uncertainty, while armed special police, clad in black, loaded them onto two buses parked in the courtyard. A few of the people boarding the buses looked longingly out of the yard. I felt a chill come over me. The mass arrests had reached Urumchi.

In the month afterward, news of the arrests spread via word of mouth. Each day, from every part of the city, hundreds of Uyghurs were called in to dozens of police stations and sent to "study." We understood by then that the "study centers" were concentration camps. People were summoned by phone to the neighborhood committee office or the police station, told simply that they would be going to "study," and taken away. One after another, I heard of friends and acquaintances who had been taken.

On an afternoon in late May, I was heading to Xinjiang Television Station to take care of some business when I received a phone call from a young writer I was close with. Just then he had been called in to the police station and told he would be sent to "study." He heard from the police, though, that if an officer would guarantee him, he could avoid being sent. Now he was calling everyone he knew to find a police officer, but he had so far been unable to find a single cop to vouch for him. He asked if I could help.

"I only know the cops who arrested and questioned me," I told him. He was silent for a moment. "OK, then, sorry to bother you." He hung up. The next day I heard he had been sent to "study."

From what I heard, in Urumchi as in Kashgar, the mass arrests first targeted devout individuals, people who had been abroad, and those with livelihoods outside the state system. The scope of the arrests then gradually expanded to other targets as well. It remained a mystery, though, how the authorities determined who would be taken. Anyone who asked why they had been arrested would be told by the police only that "your name was on the list they sent down." There was no way to know if or when your name would show up on the list. We all lived within this frightening uncertainty.

Chatting with some friends at Almas's store one day, the conversation turned to the lists. One of our friends, a bit of a computer whiz, told us these forms were very likely generated by a specially designed computer program. And it was true that there had been much talk lately of a terrifying networked police system.

We had heard that beginning late last year, everyone's data was being entered into a system known as the Integrated Joint Operations Platform. On the basis of this data, the police—and especially the neighborhood police—marked the file of each individual they considered dangerous. Since everyone's ID cards were linked via the internet to the Integrated Joint Operations Platform, anyone with a mark in their file would set off the siren when they scanned their ID card at the ubiquitous police checkpoints, and would be apprehended on the spot. Uyghurs called these marks "dots." If someone was detained due to their file being marked, people would say they were "arrested because they had a dot." More and more people had been discovering of late that these dreadful dots had been applied to them as well.

Typically, if the police arrested someone, the authorities were required by law to inform the person's family. If, as often happened, this legal requirement was ignored, family members would inquire at the police station as to why the individual had been detained and where they were being kept. If the individual was being held for a political crime—a category that for Uyghurs had been expanding year after year—the police would of course not acknowledge it, but they would at least relay where they were being kept. With the permission of the police, family members would send the detained person necessities like soap, towels, undergarments, and toilet paper. They could even meet with the prisoner. But as the mass arrests progressed, it became apparent that things were different now. There was no way to learn which "study center" detained people had been sent to. They simply vanished.

A couple of weeks into the mass internments, the husband of one of Marhaba's friends was called in to the neighborhood committee and taken away to "study." When Marhaba's friend went to the neighborhood committee in search of her husband, she was told to go ask at the police station. When she went to the police station, she was told to inquire at the district police department. The district police department refused to let her enter. Along with other distraught people who had come to inquire about their detained loved ones, she stood for three days in front of the police department, to no avail. On the third day, she heard that numerous detainees were being held in a massive camp at

Miquan, outside Urumchi. The next morning she took a photocopy of her husband's ID card and caught a taxi to Miquan. Because so many people had come in search of their family members, the police had ordered them to form a line to make inquiries. She walked to the back of the hundred-meter queue. Since the camp had been freshly built in the middle of an empty field, there was no shade in sight. After she had stood for nearly ten hours in the scorching sun, it was evening by the time her turn came. The police officer responsible for inquiries entered her husband's ID number into the computer. Her husband wasn't there, he told her.

That night, she posted to her WeChat friend circle a photo of people waiting in line outside the camp. Her caption read: "I came today in hopes that you were here, but after a day of waiting I found no trace of you. Your dear daughter stares longingly at the door. Your brave son dries my tears and comforts me. We miss you. Where could you be?"

After the mass arrests began, every time I drove past the police station I made a point of looking in at the courtyard. I couldn't drive too slowly without arousing the police's attention, so I would catch only a glimpse of the Uyghurs waiting in the courtyard to be taken for "study." I would feel the urge to take a closer look, to see if anyone I knew was among them, but I was afraid to open the car window. Although the mass arrests had persisted in Urumchi for more than a month at this point, none of my close relatives had yet been arrested. At this point, my direct experience of the arrests was only these cautious glances out my car window.

. . .

Even as the danger grew, life continued. One day around noon, I walked out of our apartment courtyard to buy some naan. Since the bakeries in our neighborhood had been shuttered, we had to pay somewhat more for naan at one of the small Uyghur-run grocery stores. As I entered a store I went to frequently, I saw two young Uyghur men chatting as they paid their bill.

"Oh, yeah, did you go to the pen yesterday?"

"We did."

"How are the sheep?"

"They just stare helplessly. We took three of them out and made them bleat a bit before we took them back."

After parting with the store owner like old friends, they walked out of the store.

"Who are they?" I asked the proprietor. "What were they talking about?"

"Those kids are officers at the police department," he replied nonchalantly, not lifting his eyes from what he was doing. "They were talking about people at the study centers."

In other words, these Uyghur policemen called detained people sheep, and the camps imprisoning them pens. Tormenting those unfortunates had become a game for them. I felt a tightening deep in my stomach.

After the arrests had continued in Urumchi for more than a month,

Uyghurs with some degree of means and position began to feel that this "wind" would pass by without touching them. Such people knew they could survive this sort of state campaign through connections or money. Recently, though, there had been increasing reports of well-known people and even government officials taken from their homes in the middle of the night. Some people were simply picked up off the streets. Government employees would go to work in the morning, never to return.

Uyghurs could only hope that this terrifying "study" would come to an end after the nineteenth Communist Party Congress in October. Each party congress was accompanied by intensified security measures throughout the country, and especially in the Uyghur region.

The younger brother of a friend of mine was a technician at the television station. According to my friend, the police arrived at his brother's home after midnight to take him away. No one knew where he was being held. He was an outstanding technical worker, a core member of the team. His relatives pleaded with the television station's executives to make inquiries about him with the police. The station's executives refused, telling them that in the present delicate circumstances, they could not get involved in matters of this kind.

If such things could befall employees at important government organs like the television station, no Uyghur could truly be safe. Those who thought that the wind would not touch them found their confidence shaken. They found themselves thinking of an old Uyghur proverb: No wall can stop the wind.

SEVEN

The Key

After a hurried Monday breakfast, Aséna and Almila headed off to school. With everything going on, my head felt heavy with worry and misfortune. I lay on my side on the couch, scrolling through my friends' WeChat posts, but nothing caught my eye. I decided to listen to some *muqam*, the dozen suites that form the core of Uyghur classical music. I selected my favorite *muqam*, the Özhal, and listened as the opening words wafted over the lute's mournful stirrings.

Soon the vale of madness will embrace this aching soul of mine,
let this ruined life I lead be ruined whole one single time.

Oh wicked fate, your cruel embrace has ground me down into
the dust,
let no one find a thing of value in the dust of my decline.

Ask not to where I go, the choice is no longer my own to take,

I hand the reins of life to fate, the path I take is her design.

I had drifted into a reverie over the ancient lyrics' aching sorrow when my ringing phone dragged me back into the twenty-first century. It was Wang Bo, a Han neighborhood committee official. His committee had jurisdiction over the building where our company had its office; Wang was our office's "household cadre."

According to China's constitution, the neighborhood committee (also known as the residents' committee) was a local popular autonomous organ through which urban residents governed, trained, and served themselves; its chief, vice chief, and committee members were to be elected by residents. In reality, I had never heard of an open neighborhood committee election. Given that each neighborhood committee contained a local Communist Party branch, people simply thought of the committees as the party's local administrative organs in the cities.

Over the past three years, the neighborhood committees in the Uyghur region had suddenly grown more powerful. While previously they were neglected offices with three or four employees, they now had staffs of thirty or forty. Each neighborhood committee also had an office for the neighborhood police officer; the officer would hurry back and forth between the committee and the police station.

Most neighborhood committee employees were entrusted with households, shops, and offices falling under their committee's purview. At the direction of their superiors, they would keep tabs on these households and establishments and send reports to the neighborhood committee chiefs and the neighborhood police officer. They focused in particular on those who lived in rented homes or lacked steady employment, as well as on devout Uyghurs who said the five daily prayers, grew beards, or wore veils. It was widely believed that these reports, sent by the neighborhood committee up the chain of command, were connected to the mass internments.

Every Monday and Wednesday, Wang Bo came to inspect our office. After each inspection, he would use his cell phone to scan the QR code on the wall just inside the office door. That code contained identifying information on each of our company's employees.

Since our company did production for films, television, and ads, a lot of people came through the office. If anyone not employed at the company happened to be there when Wang Bo came by, he would ask them one by one who they were and why they had come, making sure to record their answers. We were all used to such things by then, and none of us thought much of it.

That Monday morning, Wang Bo told me over the phone that our office was locked and that he was waiting for me in front of the building. He asked me politely to come as quickly as I could to open the office door for him.

I headed downstairs and started my car. Our apartment complex had twenty-six buildings and two gates, one for pedestrians and one for vehicles. Since the previous fall, the pedestrian entrance had been locked, and people could enter only by scanning their IDs at the turnstile in the guardhouse. Day and night, guards took shifts in this structure by the gate. Any nonresident who wanted to enter the apartment complex on foot had to leave their ID with the guards. Residents with cars entered by holding a special card up to a scanner; any cars belonging to non-residents had to be registered before entering the complex. Even so, the trunk of every car was inspected on entry. I pressed my card against the scanner and drove out onto the road.

At the intersection in front of our neighborhood, a People's Convenience Police Post had been constructed several months before. Since October, these identical two-story structures had been placed every two hundred meters along all of Urumchi's streets. On the first floor of each police post, several officers took shifts. The first floor offered passersby a row of daily necessities like flashlights, sewing kits, bicycle pumps, umbrellas, bottled water, blankets, loaves of bread, and cell phone charging cables, all neatly laid out as if for an exhibition. Also arranged nearby were whistles, long wooden clubs, rubber clubs, electric prods, handcuffs, shields, and other security articles. On the second floor of each post, fifteen to twenty armed special police awaited orders. In front of each post, a police van stood ready twenty-four hours a day.

After these police posts were built under the slogan of "providing convenience to the people," I paid close attention to them. Once, under the pretense of asking for directions, I even went inside one to take a look. But I'd never encountered anyone sincerely entering one of these police posts to ask for help. In truth, everyone knew perfectly well that these posts were part of the vast system of control and suppression directed at Uyghurs. When Uyghurs walked past these posts, they would act as if they didn't see them and avoid them as much as possible. Yet we were getting used to them, as we realized there was no escaping the omnipresent surveillance. I watched the post now as I drove past.

As I passed the Bahuliang police station on Unity Road, I glanced at the station courtyard. Two police officers were speaking to ten or so Uyghurs in front of the building. I assumed the officers were telling them that they were being sent to "study." In any event, the mass arrests seemed to have slowed after peaking for a month. Only later did we learn that this lull was temporary.

Driving past the number 10 bus line's Porcelain Factory stop, I saw that special police officers had stopped two young Uyghurs on the sidewalk and were checking their phones. Since the violent events of 2009, such things had become routine.

The previous autumn, I had been driving down Prosperity Street when I took a wrong turn. Traffic police emerged from the side of the road and cut me off, and I pulled over. The officer asked for my license. I handed it over and asked what I had done wrong. He ignored me and walked back toward his car.

I followed him, repeating my question. I must have raised my voice without knowing it, for in the blink of an eye four Han special police officers who had been patrolling the street ran up to us and brusquely asked what was going on. I explained the situation, but they had no intention of listening. Their sergeant interrupted me. "Hand me your phone!" I handed it over. "Unlock it." I unlocked it. He removed a scanning device from his pocket. Attached to one end of the device were five cables, one each for iPhones, Androids, and other types of cell phones I wasn't familiar with. He attached my iPhone to the device, pressed a button on the device's screen, and began scanning.

In the south of the Uyghur region, police had for several years been inspecting cell phones and arresting people on the basis of their contents, but the practice had only begun in Urumchi the previous fall. Since then, everyone had become very careful. People were being arrested for having downloaded "illegal" apps like the file-sharing service Zapya, or because police found "contraband" material on their phones: Quran verses, images related to Islam or to Uyghur nationalism, or even songs that the government had outlawed. It was exceedingly difficult to determine the scope of prohibited materials; these matters were governed not by law but by policy, and the policies changed constantly. Smartphones had only recently become popular in the region, and many people unaccustomed to using them had been arrested for materials they didn't even realize were on their phones.

As the situation worsened, like many others I spent hours "cleaning" my phone, much as I had cleaned my computer three years before. One by one, I deleted pictures, videos, audio recordings, and even chat logs from QQ and WeChat. I got rid of anything the police might seize on as "evidence," a category that included anything related to the Uyghur people or to Islam. All that was left on my phone were the most mundane items. But while I knew my phone contained nothing that could reasonably serve the police as a pretext, I was still a bit anxious as the officer scanned my phone. It was entirely possible for the police to use any excuse at all, or even to dispense with pretext altogether, and take me away.

The officer's device finally finished scanning my phone. The scan must not have turned up any contraband material; the officer looked puzzled and hesitated for a moment, knitting his brow. He began the scan again, averting his eyes from me. I waited, reciting to myself a poem I had written the previous year.

Patience

They stare:

the sun at the earth

lightning at a tree

a tiger at a gazelle

the night at the day

time at a river

God at man

a gun at a chest

This, then, is patience

Undefeated, merciless, eternal

The officer's scan once again failed to produce any banned content. I will never forget the look of disappointment on his face when he finally handed the phone back to me.

I thought about all of this as I drove. Our office was in an old six-story building on Unity Road, near Döngköwrük and the Grand Bazaar at the center of the old city's Uyghur districts. The building had originally housed the Autonomous Region Film Distribution Company; now it rented out space to Uyghur-owned film, television, advertisement, and media companies. Several well-known Uyghur entertainers also kept offices there.

Wang Bo presided over our building's maneuvers against violent terrorists. When he gave the order, the security guards at the front entrance would promptly blow their whistles, and from all the companies and offices in the building a gaggle of owners and office managers would come running down the stairs. Within three minutes we would be standing in formation on the plaza in front of the building. Reading from a list in Chinese, Wang Bo would call each of our names to check attendance. Sometimes, at Wang Bo's direction, we would form into military-style columns and jog over to the courtyard of the neighboring electronics pavilion, where we would join the people renting space in that building in forming a Big Line of Defense Against Violent Terrorists. While we were running from one courtyard to another, we could see the mixed feelings in the faces of people passing us on the street.

In reality, there wasn't much to these maneuvers. The cadres would consider their work successful if all the required people from the two buildings showed up with a serious attitude and urgent bearing. The entire purpose of these activities, it seemed, was to keep us in a constant state of tension and fear.

Officials from higher up would regularly come to observe, upon which our maneuvers would grow even more urgent and rigorous. If anyone failed to cooperate or took part only passively, their name would be forwarded to the neighborhood police. At a time when everyone in the building had frequent need of the neighborhood police, no one could afford to take lightly any activities organized by the neighborhood committee.

If people were forced to continue such activities, it would be only a matter of time before they would begin feeling themselves to be police, with a taste for watching and reporting on each other. They would remain constantly at the ready to confront unspecified enemies, and at the same time often feel that they themselves were enemies. After the mass arrests reached Urumchi in late April, though, the building largely emptied out and the maneuvers ceased.

Although there were few people left in the building, security measures on the premises remained at full strength. Late the previous year, walk-through metal detectors had begun to be installed in all of Urumchi's buildings, down to the public toilets. Our office building was no exception, and a walk-through scanner was set up by the entrance. Two Uyghur guards were responsible for watching it.

I met Wang Bo in front of our building, and we walked in together. Wang sauntered confidently through the scanner as if he were walking through his own front door. While I could never suppress my discomfort on passing through the device, the blank stares of the guards invariably made me wonder if it actually worked. As far as I knew, the scanner had not detected a single dangerous item in the half-year since its installation. Its real function was intimidation.

Our company's office was on the fifth floor. I opened the door for Wang Bo. He walked into the office, took out his phone, and scanned the QR code on the wall as he had many times before. Then, as he always did, he took a look through the premises. It was a big office, with three main rooms. Wang Bo, usually so assiduous in questioning any new people who showed up in our office, by now registered no surprise that none of the people on his list, none of the people he had been monitoring, were in the office anymore.

For a month now, work at the company had come to a halt: our partnership with the television station had lapsed; preparations for film production had ceased; advertisements ready to be filmed had been abandoned. All of this had happened suddenly. Some of our employees had been ordered by the police to return to the hometowns where they were still registered; others remained in Urumchi, unsure of what to do. With the company's work at a standstill, I was unable to continue employing them or paying their salaries. Wang Bo knew all this, but he continued coming twice a week to inspect the office.

"Wang Bo," I said, "you know as well as I do that our company no longer has any work or any people. From now on I'll be staying home myself. What should we do?"

"I know, I know," he responded amiably, "but you also know that I have to do my job."

"How about this," I said decisively. "You take the key. Then you can come inspect my office whenever you like."

He looked a bit taken aback, and I realized he must have thought I was mocking him. I quickly added, "Don't think twice about it. This will be more convenient for both of us. There's nothing to worry about in this office, anyway. I've moved all the important equipment to my brother's warehouse."

Wang Bo heard the sincerity in my voice. "All right, then. Let's do it."

I gave him a key to the office. Now I had one less burden.

As I walked down the stairs, I found myself thinking of a popular slogan from the 1970s: "Our all belongs to the party!" As of today, my office belonged to the party.

EIGHT

The Police Station Basement

Our daughters told us they wanted to go to Turpan to pick mulberries over the weekend. Turpan is famous for its hot weather and its grapes; in the spring it attracts visitors with its apricots and mulberries. It was already late May, and the mulberry season would soon be over. Aséna and Almila liked to pluck them from the branch and eat them on the spot; sometimes they'd climb up the mulberry trees.

Marhaba and I agreed immediately to the trip. The winter cold still hadn't left Urumchi; a couple of days enjoying Turpan's warm spring weather would be good for our heavy hearts. On a Saturday morning, the four of us piled into the car and headed for Turpan.

To pass the time on long car trips, Marhaba and I usually chatted about friends, family, travel. Given the events of the last couple of months, though, our conversations now inevitably wandered back to the political situation. These discussions generally went around in circles, with the result that conversation had become an unpleasant exercise.

As we drove toward Turpan, we discussed again whether we should leave the country. I stressed that the situation could continue to worsen, but Marhaba remained reluctant about the idea of going abroad.

"Things can't get that bad," she would often say. "God help us. We haven't done anything they could arrest us for."

It is no easy thing to leave your homeland in your forties and start life anew in a foreign country. We were doing all right in Urumchi. We had started our own company, small though it was. In sixteen years of marriage, we had together dealt with all kinds of challenges. We had bought a house, raised two kids. It hadn't been all that long since we'd established ourselves comfortably. Besides, my wife cherished our traditional way of life, and had no desire to leave her relatives and friends.

For me, as a poet, it was likewise a difficult proposition to leave my main readers behind, to live in a foreign land and learn a foreign language. The Uyghur diaspora was relatively small, as would be the readership for any works written in the diaspora. The Chinese government had long banned the import of Uyghur works published abroad; these controls would be even stricter now.

During my sophomore year of college in Beijing, I had enrolled in a two-semester English course. Early in the second semester, the Tiananmen student movement began, and we all ditched class to take part in the protests. My English remained at that one-semester level. Although later I resolved on several occasions to pick it back up and truly learn the language, something else always came up, and my plans never came to fruition. Perhaps I had never really needed to do it. If I were to go abroad now, language would prove my first and biggest problem. I would learn the language out of necessity, of course, but as I approached fifty, the idea of learning a new language well enough to write original work seemed like a fairy tale.

While Marhaba and I had never spoken openly about it, we both knew that if we left our homeland we might never be able to return. Unease and uncertainty hovered over these conversations.

Our two girls, who had long since tired of these endless discussions, had fallen asleep in the back seat. Below the Heavenly Mountains to our right, Salt Lake shone like a giant mirror tossed into the desert.

We passed through Dawanching and the road rose into the mountains. My cell phone rang through the car speakers. It was an unknown number. These days everyone feared unknown numbers.

I answered the phone. "Hello?"

"Hello. Is this Tahir Hamut *aka*?" The young woman on the phone addressed me respectfully.

"Yes, speaking."

"This is Güljan from the neighborhood committee."

"Oh, how are you doing?"

"I'm doing well, *aka*. Is your wife's name Marhaba Sabir?"

"That's right."

"*Aka*, I'm calling to let you know that the police station is taking fingerprints from everyone who has been abroad. Could you and your wife please come by the station?"

"We're actually heading to Turpan to take care of something. We'll be back tomorrow, *singlim*." Following Uyghur custom, I addressed her warmly as "younger sister."

"Hmm, in that case, please come in on Monday."

"OK, we'll head over at eight o'clock Monday morning, right when things open."

"I'm sure it will be crowded in the morning, why don't you come at two in the afternoon?"

"All right. Seems like you're working even over the weekend?"

"Yes, we've been working weekends for a while."

"OK, then. Goodbye for now."

"Goodbye."

Güljan, a Uyghur woman around twenty-five years old, had only recently begun working at the neighborhood committee that oversaw our apartment complex. She was responsible for keeping tabs on our apartment building, just as Wang Bo was for our office building. Twice a week, she would visit our apartment for an inspection. Each time she would begin by asking whether our family had any difficulties, and would then ask whether any guests had come to stay, whether any children had been born outside the state birth quota, and whether anyone in the household performed daily prayers. She would record our answers in her notebook. Meanwhile, she would look discreetly around the house. In truth, we couldn't hide anything from her.

We treated Güljan respectfully. Marhaba, always gregarious, would ask during each visit how she was doing. Güljan had finished university in 2014, but over the past three years had been unable to find employment in her field. In this, she was far from unusual. With discrimination and suspicion toward Uyghurs on the rise, numerous young Uyghur university graduates found themselves excluded from jobs commensurate with their education. While Güljan's new position at the neighborhood committee was demanding and the pay was meager, if she worked hard and passed the civil service exam she would become a career civil servant. This was her fondest wish.

We would sometimes see her, blue binder clasped under her arm, waiting for someone in front of the building, or coming and going from other families' apartments. Other times we would run into her at night in the vicinity of the building. "It's not easy for these poor souls, either," Marhaba would often sigh. At the government's encouragement, many young people like Güljan worked for the neighborhood committees.

Photos and contact information for household cadres and neighborhood police officers were posted by the doors of residential buildings, along with a reminder that we could contact them at any time "if there was anything to share." It was a not-so-subtle incentive for neighbors to observe and report on each other. Every time I entered the building, I found my gaze drawn to the photos of our neighborhood police officer and household cadre. I felt I could hear them saying, "We're always watching."

We emerged from the mountains and drove up to the Parche Saqal police checkpoint.

Driving along our designated lane, we entered the checkpoint. Marhaba got out of the car and walked over to the inspection building to scan her ID. The girls and I remained in the car. The special police officers waved the car in front of me through without inspection; I figured the driver must be Han.

Inching forward, I lowered all the windows as required and stopped the car next to the officer. With a supercilious gesture, he adjusted the machine gun strapped to his shoulder and took my ID. Comparing my face to the photo on my ID card, he asked in Chinese where I was going and for what purpose. I told him. He peered inside the car, where my two girls were now awake. Then he pointed to the trunk and told me to get out and open it, after which he leaned over and looked through the trunk. Finally, he returned my ID and motioned us onward.

I stopped the car in the large lot next to the checkpoint and waited for Marhaba. After ten minutes or so she emerged from the inspection building. "I'm so tired of all their crap," she muttered as she lowered herself into the car.

Our weekend vacation in Turpan passed under a cloud of anxiety. As hard as we tried to enjoy ourselves, we couldn't put our Monday appointment at the police station out of our minds. "They don't want anything besides our fingerprints, right?" asked Marhaba. "I don't think they do," I said. "If there were anything else, they would have told us to drop everything and come immediately." By "anything," Marhaba meant being sent to "study."

We returned to Urumchi on Sunday night. On Monday, a bit before two, Marhaba and I made our way to the police station. The gate was locked. A middle-aged Uyghur sentry in the guardhouse asked what we had come for, and in a notebook recorded my name, ethnicity, and ID

number, as well as the number of people I was with. Then he opened the
small automatic door leading into the courtyard.

When we stepped inside the police station, a young Han officer at a
desk in the front hall asked why we had come. In the registry book in
front of him, he also took down my name, ethnicity, and ID number,
and recorded the number of people I was with. "Head down to the basement," he said, pointing us to the door at the top of the basement stair-
way. I felt my blood run cold.

Three years earlier, in 2014, I had come to this police station to take
care of some passport paperwork for Marhaba and our daughters. After
combing through our family's digital files, our neighborhood police officer deemed the three of them eligible to receive passports. The passport application form then needed to be signed by the police station's
deputy chief for national security. The deputy chief at this station was a
Kazakh named Erbol.

Standing in this very hall, I had asked the officer on duty where I
could find Erbol. The Han officer told me to wait there, as Erbol was
currently questioning someone in the basement.

I had taken a seat on the iron bench in the corridor and waited. After
a little while, I heard a man's voice crying out wretchedly from the basement. It sounded to me like a middle-aged Uyghur man's voice. I shuddered. The officer on duty hurried over and firmly shut the metal door
leading down to the basement. Typically, basement stairways didn't
have doors like this. It was clear that this police station had made its
basement into an interrogation chamber.

After half an hour Erbol had emerged from the basement. Rising from the bench, I explained the situation and handed him the statement the neighborhood police officer had prepared along with the passport application form. Agitated and weary, he put his cigarette between his lips and held the form in one hand as he signed it with the other. His hand shook as he wrote his name.

Now Marhaba and I walked through that metal doorway and descended the stairs to the basement. The staircase let out into a corridor about twenty meters long. To the left were three cells, separated from the corridor by metal bars.

In the first cell stood a heavy iron "tiger chair," used for interrogating and torturing prisoners. The iron restraint used for strapping prisoners' chests to the chair hung open, and the iron rings for securing hands and feet dangled on either side. The chair looked as if it were waiting for the next unfortunate soul to sit in it. Along the walls, iron rings were affixed to the concrete floor; I figured these were for shackling people. In the middle of the floor were faded bloodstains. The cells were empty, their doors open.

On the right was a row of five offices, each with a large window facing the corridor. When we entered the basement, two husband-and-wife couples were waiting their turn. Before long, twenty-some other people had queued up behind us. Nearly all of them were middle-aged Uyghurs; from their appearance, it was clear they were relatively well off. But their faces were clouded by worry and confusion.

We followed the queue into the second office, where we found Güljan sitting behind a desk. She had us sign a registry. When she had called us on Saturday, she had told us the police station needed to take our fingerprints. Now she told us that in addition to our fingerprints, the police would be taking our blood samples, voice prints, and facial images. Marhaba looked at me anxiously when she heard this. "Let them take what they will from us," I whispered to her, "as long as we get out of here safely."

In this office our blood samples would be taken by a young Uyghur woman, likely a neighborhood committee cadre, and a young Uyghur man, a police assistant. When I asked why they hadn't invited a nurse, the police assistant indifferently retorted, "Come on, this is easy stuff!" The young woman clumsily took blood samples from our index fingers.

We walked down the corridor to the first office, where police officers would be taking samples of our voices, collecting our fingerprints, and scanning our faces.

First, I picked up the copy of the *Urumchi Evening Gazette* laid out on a table and walked over to the microphone. As I read one of the articles, I deliberately spoke like a professional announcer, in the Uyghur language's most formal register. I figured this would at least make it a bit harder for the police to identify my voice from the sample. I never spoke that way in daily life. After two minutes, the technician who took my voice sample gestured for me to stop. She gave me a satisfied smile, as if to say, "You read that beautifully," and saved the file.

Fingerprints were next. Following the technician's instructions, I placed my hands one at a time on the scanner, my fingers splayed. Then I had to roll each finger over the scanner, ensuring that all fingers' prints were fully recorded. If a scan did not meet the computer's requirements, the system would reject it and I would have to redo that finger. Scanning all ten fingers to this standard was no easy task. For some fingers, I had to repeat the scanning procedure multiple times.

My fingerprints had been taken a number of times in my life, but I had never seen or even heard of a fingerprinting process as exhaustive as the one I underwent that day. Although the process was extremely tedious, I realized when it was over that with my usual perfectionism I had been utterly focused on getting the scans done correctly.

Now it was time for facial imaging. A Han police assistant motioned me over to a chair facing a camera. He adjusted the tripod so the lens was level with my face.

I had been a film director for eighteen years, and had seen and used cameras of all shapes and sizes. Following the 2009 violence in Urumchi, surveillance equipment had been installed in every corner of the city, and I had subsequently encountered all manner of security cameras. But this was a camera unlike any I had seen. Running from one end to the other was a flat lens about three centimeters high and twenty centimeters long.

The woman operating the computer explained what I was to do. At the signal, I needed to look straight at the camera for two seconds, then turn my head slowly and steadily to the right. After two seconds in that position, I was then to turn at the same speed back to face the camera for another two seconds, then repeat the same motion to the left. At the same slow, steady speed, I then had to tilt my head back and look up for two seconds, after which I was to lower my head and look straight at the camera for two seconds, following which I had to tilt my head down and repeat the same motion. Finally, I had to look straight at the camera, slowly and completely open my mouth, and hold that position for two seconds. After I closed my mouth and looked steadily at the camera for a further two seconds, my facial scan would be complete. All of these movements needed to be completed in the assigned order in a single, uninterrupted sequence. If any movement did not conform to the requirements, the computer's scanning program would give a signal and stop running, after which I would have to start over from the beginning. I successfully completed the sequence on my third try.

The sense of dread filling the police station basement made one forget how absurd and comical all of these motions were. Anyone summoned to this basement could think of nothing but finishing and leaving as quickly as possible.

Marhaba, who had been going through these procedures immediately after me, struggled when she came to the facial scan. As hard as she tried, she couldn't maintain the steady speed required. Her movements would be too fast, then they would be too slow. Her face reddened with frustration and resentment. I stood to the side, encouraging and prompting her. I noticed my palms were sweaty from the tension.

The facial scanning sequences for men and women differed in only one way. While men were required to open their mouths wide at the end of the sequence, women had to close their mouths tightly and puff out their cheeks. I wondered what the reason was for this difference, but to this day I haven't been able to figure it out.

After trying again and again to complete the sequence, on her sixth attempt Marhaba finally succeeded. We couldn't help but feel as happy as kids. We were finally done with everything.

We returned to the other office and reported to Güljan that we had finished all of the procedures. Then we made our way through the weary line of people waiting their turn and headed upstairs.

As we climbed the stairs, I muttered half-jokingly to Marhaba, "Now the surveillance cameras will be able to recognize us from behind."

It was past five o'clock by the time we left the police station.

"We need to leave the country," Marhaba said bitterly.

Your Unknown Place

Here people's names were not contagious,

we said they were, it came to be.

There was no sand here growing roots,

we said there was, it came to be.

Here time did not drip from the walls,

we said it did, it came to be.

Here loneliness did not multiply,

we said it did, it came to be.

Here a thousand eyes did not fleck the skies,

we said they did, it came to be.

Here there were no fugitive forgettings,

we said there were, it came to be.

Yet our words could undo nothing here,

even the things we brought to be.

NINE

Passports

W e had never even thought of going abroad.

After more than a dozen years, I still felt the wound left by my last attempt to leave the country. My unrealized plans had led to the most difficult period of my life. Following my arrest at the border and the three years I spent in prison, I had ceased to have any thought of passports and visas.

One day in late 2012, though, I was chatting with a businessman who had come to our office to have a television ad filmed. He mentioned to me that proprietors of private companies could apply for passports using their companies' documentation; this was how he had obtained his own passport. It occurred to me that since I had the opportunity, I might as well get a passport. If circumstances permitted, I could go sightseeing abroad.

In the Uyghur community, a passport was something momentous.

Having been isolated and politically constricted for many years, Uyghurs saw a passport as a precious letter of admission to the outside world. The vast majority of Uyghurs never laid eyes on one. For the most part, passports belonged only to prosperous merchants who did business abroad.

In early 2013, I applied for a passport with my company's documents. Around this time, as China's ties to the rest of the world continued to deepen, the Chinese government streamlined the passport application process. For Han, it was now a matter of bringing one's ID card to the relevant office and filling out the application form. For Uyghurs and many other minority citizens, however, applying for a passport remained a long, complex, and arduous process. As a business owner in the regional capital, I faced fewer obstacles in obtaining a passport than most Uyghurs; even so, I had to fight through maddening layers of bureaucracy.

After carefully filling out the eight-page passport application form, I prepared my company's work certification. Stamped with the company's seal, this document listed my responsibilities at the company, my monthly salary, the reason I needed a passport, the dates I planned to be abroad, the destination country, my reason for traveling there, and the company's guarantee that I would return by the specified date. These travel details were a formality; there was no need for them to be accurate or exact.

Since I owned my own company, I wrote out the certification myself and didn't need to go begging anyone for a stamp. After preparing the certification precisely to standard, I picked up my company seal, pressed it vigorously into the red ink, and stamped it with relish on the document.

For the vast majority of Uyghurs who didn't own companies, it was exceedingly difficult to obtain one of these guarantees. I had produced several such documents in my own company's name to help trusted friends apply for passports. Needless to say, this was not without risk. If someone I had provided a guarantee for was arrested during the passport application process or at the border, the police could swiftly come for me as well. Fortunately, such a situation had never arisen.

I took the application materials to our neighborhood policewoman's office. Adile was a Uyghur woman in her mid-thirties. She looked carefully through my passport application form, then inspected one by one our company's business license and organization code certificate, our local and national tax licenses, my ID card, our family's household registration, and my company's guarantee. Then, after turning to her computer and looking through the police station's file on me, she prepared a document reading, "By investigation we have confirmed that our resident Tahir Hamut has no criminal record, that he is not among the 'seven kinds of people prohibited from traveling abroad,' and that he did not participate in the 2009 Urumchi incident. He is eligible to receive a passport." She signed the printout and handed it to me. I brought the document to Erbol, the deputy station chief. After reviewing it, he took my passport application form and in the indicated space wrote "I agree" in Chinese before signing his name. I then walked over to the police station's administrative office, where the station's official seal was stamped over Erbol's signature.

I took the completed application to the neighborhood committee and received a one-page form entitled "Inspection and Comment Form for Urumchi City Residents Traveling Abroad." After filling it out, I took the form back to the neighborhood committee and then to the sector committee for approval and more red stamps.

The final blank space on this form required the stamp of the Tengri-tagh District National and Religious Affairs Office. To obtain this, my company needed to affix its own stamp to a guarantee stating that I would make no unauthorized pilgrimages to Mecca, and that the company would bear full responsibility if I did. Among the many stamps needed to procure a passport, only the stamp for this guarantee and for the work certification belonged to me. In a situation where any one of these innumerable stamps—the symbols of authority in China—could decide one's fate, it meant something to have even one stamp to myself.

I took the guarantee to the National and Religious Affairs Office for the final stamp on my form. In total, the process had taken about two weeks.

I looked at the succession of round red stamps on the form. Some were a vivid crimson, with the Chinese and Uyghur scripts clearly legible. Some were faint, with the script inside impossible to read; but these stamps were still crucial. I slipped the form carefully into a folder. It was a relief to have all the bureaucracy taken care of. I felt lighter.

Gathering the two forms, my identification materials, and my company's documents, I headed to the service center of the District Public Security Bureau's Border Control Office. The responsible officer took my materials and examined them thoroughly, before telling me that they would call me once the national security unit had concluded its examination. I had heard that if your materials were approved by the national security unit, your passport application would be successful.

After around ten days, I received a call from the District Public Security Bureau asking me to pick up my materials, which I then brought to the City Public Security Bureau. After waiting my turn for two hours at the bureau's Border Control Office, I handed the materials to the employee at the window.

Exactly thirty days later, I received my passport.

Given Uyghurs' increasing marginalization in our own homeland, Marhaba and I had long worried about our daughters' futures. It was hard to be optimistic. "What's happened to us has happened," we would say to each other, "but our girls' prospects shouldn't be so dark." Even if our daughters graduated from China's top universities, as Uyghurs they would inevitably face constant discrimination in their careers and in daily life.

Around this time, we learned that some affluent Uyghur acquaintances of ours had sent their children to study in American high schools. Following some family discussion, we decided to begin preparing for Aséna and Almila to study abroad. To begin with, Aséna would take a year off from school to study English full-time. Our plan was to send her to the United States as soon as she finished middle school. Marhaba and I resolved to work as hard as we could to save money and ensure our daughters an education abroad.

Now it was time to obtain passports for Marhaba and the girls. Unless they owned their own businesses, Uyghurs and other minority citizens had to obtain a letter of invitation from abroad in order to apply for a passport. Once Marhaba and our daughters obtained such a letter, they would need to navigate the same bureaucratic maze that I had.

For the invitation letter, Marhaba and I considered each one of our friends and acquaintances abroad. It had to be someone reliable; in other words, someone who was a citizen of the country they lived in, who wanted to help us, and who was not on the Chinese government's blacklist. The invitation letter had to clearly state the inviter's name, citizenship, and address, as well as the invited party's name, birth date, ID number, and intended time of visit. In addition, the letter had to guarantee that the inviter would take responsibility for the visitor's expenses during their trip. The envelope had to bear the invited party's home address in Chinese.

We decided that our best option was to ask our friends Mirshat and Gülnar, a couple who lived in Sweden and had taken Swedish citizenship. Mirshat was a writer whom I knew from literary circles; Gülnar and I had been classmates in college, and had later worked briefly at the same school in Urumchi. They were eager to help, and Gülnar volunteered to take care of it herself.

Once we received Gülnar's invitation, protocol required that we have it officially translated from English to Chinese. Then, after several weeks gathering paperwork, filling out forms, and acquiring red stamps, I took the invitation, the application form, and the other materials to the service center of the District Public Security Bureau's Border Control Office. The Han police officer flipped through the materials and announced that I needed to provide evidence that Gülnar had renounced her Chinese citizenship. I replied that Gülnar had already become a citizen of Sweden. But the officer merely repeated that, according to regulations, Chinese people who took up foreign citizenship needed to carry out the official procedure for giving up their Chinese citizenship. He tossed my materials back to me. There was nothing more to say. Seething, I returned to my office.

I asked around about how one could officially annul one's Chinese citizenship. Apparently, a direct relative could carry out the citizenship renunciation process on Gülnar's behalf. I left Gülnar a detailed voice message on WeChat explaining all of this.

I heard back from Gülnar the following day. Before moving abroad, she had purchased an apartment from her work unit. This apartment was still in her name, and for that reason she could not yet annul her Chinese citizenship. In other words, this wouldn't work. We needed to find someone else.

Finally, we asked a distant relative of Marhaba's in Australia to send Marhaba and our daughters an invitation to visit. We had the letter translated from English to Chinese at the expensive translation company designated by the government. I brought the materials once more to the officer. This time the materials passed successfully through the review.

After three months of laborious bureaucracy and anxious waiting, Marhaba, Aséna, and Almila's passports were issued in July. Overjoyed, we went to celebrate at one of Urumchi's finest restaurants, which served Uyghur, Turkish, and Western food. We ordered everything. Marhaba was fond of Turkish kebab, while our daughters devoured pizza with gusto. Then, at Aséna and Almila's request, we headed to the water park in the south of the city. Marhaba and I watched with delight as our daughters enjoyed one attraction after another. Then we all took a cutter around the lake. Each time the cutter zoomed into a turn, Aséna and Almila shouted to their hearts' content.

Aséna had just graduated from elementary school. In September, when the new school year began, she registered at our local junior high. In accordance with our preparations for Aséna to study abroad, I procured a note from a doctor acquaintance, claiming that Aséna had experienced sudden hearing loss in her left ear and required treatment. I went to meet the school's Han principal and with some difficulty got his approval for Aséna to stay home for treatment.

We hired a tutor to teach Aséna English. After a couple of months, I visited her school principal again with another note from my doctor acquaintance: "There has been no measurable improvement in Aséna's condition; she requires further treatment." The principal was incensed. "What kind of illness is this, with no improvement after two months?" Even so, after I explained the situation with all the pathos I could muster, he consented to Aséna taking the year off and repeating the grade the following year. With her school situation resolved, Aséna threw herself into her English studies.

...

On September 23, 2014, the Urumchi Intermediate People's Court found Ilham Tohti guilty of the crime of separatism and sentenced him to life in prison. Every Uyghur intellectual was deeply shaken by the news.

Days later, I headed to Beijing. My alma mater, Central University for Nationalities, was celebrating the tenth anniversary of the Uyghur Language and Literature Section's elevation to a full-fledged department. I was invited to attend the event along with a number of other Uyghur graduates who had achieved some measure of professional success. Most of us knew each other already. In addition to the department's festivities, a number of us presented scholarly papers at the event. Marhaba, who had never been to Beijing, joined me on the trip. She wanted to see the city, and especially the university where I had studied. I felt a surge of pride introducing my wife to my former professors.

While I enjoyed the festivities, Ilham's recent life sentence was never far from my thoughts. Two visits from friends in Beijing underlined the gravity of the situation.

One friend, a Beijing-based Han writer who had long been concerned about Uyghur rights, had been with Ilham when he called me on New Year's Day a couple of years earlier. Now he told us in detail about Ilham's arrest, and especially about the difficult situation in which Ilham's wife and children now found themselves. When we expressed interest in visiting them, our friend dissuaded us. Ilham's family was under surveillance, he explained, with plainclothes officers taking shifts in front of their apartment building day and night.

On the second day of the event, a former classmate from my Beijing days came by our hotel in the evening. After asking me to join him outside so that we could speak privately, he told me that my friend Jüret had sent his greetings from the United States, and had given him a message for me: we must leave for America immediately. Having finished his doctoral studies in Japan, Jüret had left for America with his family the year before and had received asylum. He was deeply worried about the rapid deterioration of conditions for Uyghurs in China. Wary of saying any of this to me over the phone, he had relayed the message through my classmate, who had recently visited the United States.

Although since Ilham's arrest I had sometimes entertained the idea of going abroad, I had never given the matter sustained and serious consideration. But Jüret had spoken the truth. Things were growing ever more precarious for Uyghurs in China, and Uyghur intellectuals faced particular danger. It was time to do some serious thinking.

TEN

Rejection

Ilham Tohti's life sentence for "splitting the fatherland" had shaken me deeply. To be safe, I resolved to apply for American visas for our family. As for moving abroad, Marhaba and I agreed we would continue thinking about it and watching how the situation unfolded. American tourist visas for Chinese citizens had been extended to ten years; we figured we would have plenty of time to make our decision if things looked bad.

Asking around, we found a visa agent in Beijing, a young Han man named Li Yang who ran a small travel agency near the embassy district. Li struck me as friendly and experienced, and he told me he had helped a number of Uyghurs procure visas. He had a fair understanding of the situation in Xinjiang and of the circumstances Uyghurs currently faced. I was pleased that I had found the right person to help us.

After I paid the US visa application fee and the fee for Li Yang's services online, Li sent me a list of materials to collect for our applications.

I filled out the tourist visa application form and emailed it to Li, along with copies of our passports and ID cards. Li got us an interview appointment at the US embassy for March 2015.

In mid-March we prepared the materials Li Yang told us we might need for the visa interview: our passports and ID cards, our household registration book, the deed to our apartment, a bank balance statement, our marriage license, our daughters' birth certificates, our company's registration, my college diploma, and even the book I had published. Altogether, these materials filled a knapsack.

In addition, Marhaba and I each had to provide a written guarantee from our company. This document included our responsibilities at the company, our yearly income, the dates we intended to travel in the United States, the source of funds for our trip, and the company's guarantee that we would return by the date stated.

The balance statement was to be obtained directly from the bank. It had to attest that the applicant had at least one hundred thousand yuan in currency, and to specify any transactions involving these funds over the previous six months. At an average Urumchi salary, this sum would take someone a year and a half to earn; because we were applying as a family, we had to have twice this amount in our account. We procured the documentation from the bank.

Having completed our preparations, Marhaba and I took a flight to Beijing. Once we arrived, we went directly to the Xinjiang Affairs Complex, which provides services for Xinjiang residents in the capital, and checked in to the complex's hotel. Outside of the Uyghur region, hotels in China generally would not rent rooms to people from Xinjiang, and especially not to Uyghurs. Even if they did allow a Uyghur guest to rent a room, the police had to be notified immediately. The police would then arrive swiftly at the hotel. If the guests were lucky, the police would leave after examining their ID cards and clarifying why they had come and how long they planned to stay. If they were less lucky, they would be hauled off to the police station, where the cops would question them, take their mug shots and fingerprints, and then finally let them go.

For this reason, the best hotel options for Uyghurs in Beijing were those at the Xinjiang Affairs Complex and in the vicinity of the Central University for Nationalities, where many Uyghurs studied. Since Uyghurs stayed frequently at these hotels, there were fewer issues with the authorities.

The next day, as planned, we went to Li Yang's office. His manner was warm and conscientious as he noted a few things we should pay particular attention to at the American embassy. He warned us that consular officials might ask unexpected questions with no obvious relation to our visas, like our anniversary, our children's birthdays, whether Marhaba was pregnant, or the square meterage of our house. If we were hesitant or unable to answer the questions, our applications could be denied.

He added that since ours were "blank passports" with no visas in them yet, our chances of receiving American visas were quite low. But it was still worth trying, he continued, given that our circumstances were good. By this, he meant that I owned a company and worked as a film director, that we were doing well financially, and that our household registration was in Urumchi.

I was irked to hear him say our chances at the visas were "quite low." He should have told us that at the very beginning. But then, what would it have changed if he had told us this to start with? There was no better option. Most likely we would still have chosen to give it a try.

That evening, Marhaba and I spent a couple of hours in our hotel room practicing the questions the consular official might ask.

The next day, at Li Yang's urging, we arrived at the American embassy two hours before our appointment. In front of the embassy, a line of perhaps a thousand people snaked through four rows, each a hundred meters long. Marhaba and I joined the final row.

People coming out of the embassy walked by us. Some of them trudged wearily by, white slips of paper in their hands; others grinned triumphantly as they passed, ostentatiously clasping blue slips of paper. We gathered that those whose visa applications were refused received white slips, while those with approved applications got blue ones.

After waiting in line for a couple of hours, passing through multiple layers of embassy security, and having our fingerprints taken, we came finally to a corridor where visa officials sat behind windows. Young men and women who looked to be student interns were directing applicants to different windows. Despite my best efforts to remain calm and collected, I couldn't help feeling a bit nervous. So as not to let it show, I turned my head back and smiled at Marhaba. It was no use. I could see in her eyes, directed intently at the windows ahead of us, the overwhelming hope that we would get a good official, one who would give us visas.

We could see the officers behind the three windows as they spoke with applicants. One of the officers was a balding middle-aged man, one a strongly built black-haired woman, one a young blond woman. Though I knew it was pointless, I found myself scrutinizing their appearances, facial expressions, and interactions with applicants in an effort to guess which of them would be most likely to approve our application.

Our turn came. Marhaba and I were directed over to the young blond official's window. We handed her our materials. From among our four passports she selected mine, and began carefully comparing the information in it to the files on her computer. Searching for some sign of whether she would give us a visa, I was alert to her every expression and gesture. She finished comparing the information and typed a few lines into her computer. Then she placed two white slips atop the four passports and slid them back across the counter to me. "I'm sorry," she said in Chinese. "Our visa policy is currently very strict. We are unable to give you a visa."

Though Marhaba and I had discussed this possibility many times, it was still a heavy blow to be turned down without so much as a question. For a moment I was at a loss for words. Then I tried explaining to the visa official that our daughters had their hearts set on a trip to America. Even while I was saying it, I knew how pathetic I seemed. Seeing me in this state, the woman rose from her chair and apologized repeatedly. At that point one of the interns came over and ushered us out of the building.

Marhaba and I walked defeatedly out of the embassy courtyard. I called Li Yang and told him we had been rejected. After offering some words of sympathy, he told me that if we were intent on getting

American visas, we should first visit some other developed Western countries, especially in Europe, and then patiently wait a year or so. At that point, we would stand a good chance of receiving US visas.

After returning to Urumchi, we began making inquiries about travel to Europe, eventually settling on a Uyghur tour group organized by an Urumchi travel agency. In fifteen days, the group would make the rounds of Italy, Germany, Belgium, the Netherlands, France, and Turkey. We would each receive an Italian visa. Although the tour was quite expensive, it was well worth it if we could make a trip to Europe and by doing so obtain a visa to the United States. Marhaba's parents agreed to watch Aséna and Almila while we were gone.

On the morning of April 26, Marhaba and I joined the other eighteen Uyghurs in our tour group at Diwopu International Airport in Urumchi. The travel agency had assigned a Uyghur man about my age to be our tour guide. Under his direction, we checked our bags, passed through security, and got in line for border control.

Just then, a young Uyghur pop star came hurrying up. Having carved out a distinctive style on the Uyghur music scene, this singer had recently become famous across China after placing second in a televised singing competition with his performances of Chinese songs. A decade earlier, when he had just started performing, I had produced his music videos.

When they saw him, the young Han officers busily examining us and processing our paperwork stopped what they were doing and gazed at the singer admiringly. Approaching our group, the singer greeted the others with a nod before taking my hand and telling me he was heading to Turkey for a series of concerts. The other members of his band were waiting for him in Istanbul.

Meanwhile, several female border control officers approached the singer and asked if they could take photos with him; he gamely posed for the photos. At a time when Han were taking an ever-darker view of Uyghurs, it was remarkable to see these Han officers so enamored of the singer. Because he had a first-class ticket, the singer sailed through customs in no time, and headed toward the gate without waiting in line like the rest of us.

When my turn came, I handed the officer my passport and ID card. Carefully examining my ID, he compared me to my picture, then asked me why my ID had a Beijing number despite my Urumchi address. I explained that I had received my ID card while in college in Beijing, and that the ID number had remained unchanged even after I returned to Urumchi. He must have encountered similar issues before, since he immediately saw that my explanation was reasonable. Nonetheless, such situations were unusual, especially for Uyghurs. This aroused his attention.

The officer pulled me out of the line and told me to wait in front of a nearby office. It seemed this might take a while, so I settled into a chair. The other members of the tour group looked at me. Marhaba's face was shadowed by worry and discouragement. I gave her a smile. The truth was that I felt quite calm.

The officer called another officer over, handed him my ID card, and whispered something. The second officer took my ID card and walked into the office. A minute or two later, another man from our tour group, a merchant from Yarkand, was ordered to wait with me. Radiating anxiety, he followed my lead and sat in the chair beside me.

Aside from the two of us, everyone else in our tour group had successfully passed through border control and awaited us on the other side of the checkpoint exit.

Ten or so minutes later, the officer emerged from the office with our ID cards and handed them to us without a word. Relieved, the rotund Yarkandi merchant scurried past me to the checkpoint exit.

That night we landed at Atatürk Airport in Istanbul. This was the first time Marhaba and I had set foot on foreign soil. Nineteen years earlier, my dream of studying in Istanbul had gone unfulfilled. I had paid a heavy price for that dream. Amid these thoughts, I felt a powerful excitement well up inside me alongside a wisp of regret.

"You didn't make it to Istanbul last time," said Marhaba, smiling. "Now you're finally here."

After we went through customs at the airport, our tour guide collected all of our passports. The Chinese government was deeply worried about its citizens escaping while traveling abroad. Any travel agency that allowed a tourist to escape was punished. Our tour guide therefore kept our passports throughout the trip. At times when we needed them, as when boarding a plane or purchasing something from a duty-free shop, we would ask him for our passports and return them to him afterward.

The next afternoon, we flew from Istanbul to Rome. Our tour bus took us through Rome, the Vatican, and Venice before heading out of Italy and north through Europe. In each city we passed through on our eight-day trip—Munich, Brussels, Amsterdam—we would hurriedly view a couple of the most important tourist sites and take a few photos before pressing onward. It was more a marathon than a vacation.

Many places we visited had no Uyghur restaurants; a halal restaurant of any kind was sometimes hard to find. The naan we had taken from Urumchi came in quite handy. Each night, tired and hungry, we would drag ourselves back to the hotel. Even so, we thoroughly enjoyed the trip. We were now seeing with our own eyes places we had only read about in books or viewed in films.

On the morning of May 4, we left Brussels and headed for Paris. Mirshat, Gülnar, and their children were waiting for us there. After making plans for our Europe trip, we had gotten in touch with Mirshat and Gülnar's family in Sweden, and they had arranged to fly down to Paris to meet up with us.

We arrived in Paris in the late morning. As scheduled, we visited the Louvre, and then made the rounds of some perfume stores in the area. Dinner was at Dolan Uyghur Restaurant. When our tour group entered the restaurant, we saw Mirshat and Gülnar waiting for us. Their ten-year-old son and six-year-old daughter had come with them. We embraced. In my recollection, it had been more than a decade since I had seen Mirshat and Gülnar. During that time, they had not been back to the Uyghur region, and they missed their homeland and friends. Although Gülnar and Marhaba had never met, and had only ever spoken on WeChat, they embraced like old friends, tears in their eyes. We learned later that the other members of our tour group assumed we were relatives. Our two families sat down to a meal of lamb pilaf. We had missed Uyghur food during our journey, and this Paris pilaf tasted particularly good to us.

The next morning, as planned, our tour group took a boat excursion on a downtown stretch of the Seine. The Eiffel Tower loomed nearby. A diminutive version of the Statue of Liberty stood alone on a small island. As the boat passed under one bridge after another, I thought of the great poet Paul Celan. He had been deeply influential among young Uyghur poets. Celan's remarkable poem "Death Fugue," which drew from his and other European Jews' experiences during the Nazi genocide, had to my knowledge been translated into Uyghur at least three times and had been the subject of spirited discussion on Uyghur literary forums online.

I had first encountered Celan's poetry in the early nineties. From that time, I had sought out his poetry in Chinese translation. I read and reread some of my favorite Celan poems; each time, I felt I was encountering them anew.

Celan had lived many years as an émigré in Paris and had written much of his work here. I knew that on an April day in 1970, just a few months after my own birth, he had ended his life by hurling himself from a bridge into the Seine. Perhaps it was one of the bridges we were passing under. If I had had enough time in Paris, I might have visited Paul Celan's grave.

Watching the slow currents of the Seine, I found myself thinking of Celan's poem "Memory of France."

> He left by the door, the rain followed him out.
>
> We were dead and were able to breathe.

ELEVEN

The Far Shore

Seeing Mirshat and Gülnar meant more to us than strolling the streets of Paris. That afternoon, in order to spend more time with them, we asked our tour guide for permission to leave the group for the rest of the day.

After we met up with Mirshat and Gülnar's family, we strolled around the Paris streets a bit before returning to their hotel. I took the opportunity to call my friend Jüret in the United States. Using Mirshat's phone in that Paris hotel room, Jüret and I were able to speak far more freely than we ever could have on a phone call from the Uyghur region. Jüret again urged me to leave for America. Marhaba and I had not yet made a decision about immigrating to the US, I told him; even if we chose to do so, we would first need American visas.

Afterward, we sat chatting and drinking tea with Mirshat and Gülnar in their hotel room. They told us why they had left our homeland and how they had ended up in Sweden.

Mirshat began the story, but before long Gülnar grew dissatisfied with his recounting and took over. After that, they spoke in turns, correcting and supplementing each other.

In 2002, a close associate of Mirshat's had relayed some information to a friend in Germany: their city government had been banning and burning books with religious and "ethnic" content. The friend in Germany then shared the information with Western news media. When the Chinese security organs caught wind of this, they arrested Mirshat's associate; frightened, he confessed immediately. The police told the man he could escape punishment if he exposed Uyghur cadres who opposed the state and harbored strong ethnic feelings. The first person he gave away was Mirshat.

Although Mirshat worked in a government office, in the company of friends he was—like many Uyghur intellectuals—in the habit of expressing his discontent over the trampling of Uyghurs' legal rights. On a number of occasions, he had commented that "One of these days, America will sort out China."

When the police came for Mirshat, he denied having ever spoken against the government. The police, though, revealed they had been keeping tabs on him for some time. They knew he had criticized state policy on various occasions, and they knew what he had said about America and China. When they mentioned the name of his associate, Mirshat knew he had been given away. After a harsh warning, he was released. He now knew, however, that he was under surveillance, and he and Gülnar, married only three months, decided to leave the country.

They obtained an invitation letter from friends abroad and got their passports. They then explained the situation to an uncle who was a wealthy carpet merchant; he agreed to lend them ten thousand dollars. Their plan was to head first to Kazakhstan, at the invitation of a Kazakh friend of Mirshat's. A Kazakhstan visa was relatively easy to get; once there, they would head on to Europe.

In January 2003, without informing their workplaces, they obtained tourist visas from the Kazakhstan consulate in Urumchi and took a flight to Almaty. This was their first trip abroad; the world beyond China was completely new to them. A Uyghur acquaintance in Almaty promised to procure them European visas and set them on their way; they gave him a thousand dollars. He kept them waiting for half a year, during which they were unable to go anywhere. In addition, in late March the United States invaded Iraq, following which European consulates in Kazakhstan tightened their visa policies. Mirshat and Gülnar's hope of reaching Europe from Kazakhstan grew ever dimmer. After six months, they realized their acquaintance had put one over on them.

Around then, in a sudden stroke of luck, they received a visa from the Iranian embassy in Kazakhstan. As soon as they arrived in Iran, however, they could feel China's powerful influence in the country, and they began to worry. Even when they applied for a visa from the Turkish embassy in Tehran, they were told to provide verification from the Chinese embassy. Needless to say, this was impossible.

Although they looked into various conventional ways to reach Turkey, they were ultimately left with no options but entering illegally. They began looking for refugee smugglers.

Traveling from Tehran to Tabriz, they retained the services of some Kurdish smugglers and rode by horseback for a night. From there, they joined more than fifty Pakistanis and Afghans who planned to furtively cross the border. Dressed as Kurds, they hid in the mountains by day and at night took footpaths toward the Turkish border. The hunger, thirst, and fatigue were constant. When they ran out of food, they would buy yogurt and flatbread from mountain peddlers at high prices. When they were thirsty, they drank stagnant water from puddles. Gülnar was the only woman in the entire group. On a journey that saw several strapping men collapse from exhaustion, she kept resolutely onward and gave constant encouragement to Mirshat. There was no one to help those unable to endure the hardship of the trek; when they fell behind, they were easy prey for thieves and bandits in the mountains.

At one point they came across several armed Kurdish smugglers, who confronted Mirshat: "Are you infidels?" Mirshat replied that they were Muslims. Unpersuaded, they searched Gülnar's knapsack. In it, the smugglers found Muhammad Salih Haji's Uyghur translation of the Quran, with the Arabic printed in the margins. That Quran saved Gülnar and Mirshat. Again and again, in Almaty and Tehran, belongings they had brought on their journey had been lost and pilfered; they themselves were surprised that the Quran had remained in Gülnar's knapsack all that time.

The Kurdish smugglers hated Turkey. When they heard that Mirshat and Gülnar planned to go to Turkey and that they knew Chinese, they cursed Turkey and suggested that Mirshat and Gülnar stay with them. Together, they could fill Turkey to the brim with refugees from China;

they promised to make Mirshat and Gülnar rich. Mirshat replied politely that their relatives in Turkey were waiting for them.

They walked for five nights before finally crossing the border at midnight into Turkey's Van Province. They spent the rest of the night in a cattle pen with the other refugees. The next day, for a hundred-dollar fee, the refugee smugglers punched their passports with a stamp indicating they had arrived at Atatürk Airport a week before. If Turkish gendarmes stopped them on the road, they should say they had come to visit the famous tourist destination Lake Van. With that, the smugglers sent them on their way to Istanbul.

They traveled by intercity bus, passing through numerous checkpoints along the way. Although the gendarmerie checked their passports multiple times, they didn't recognize the stamps as forgeries, perhaps because the passports themselves were genuine. Finally, they arrived safely in Istanbul.

Although Uyghur acquaintances in Istanbul made Mirshat and Gülnar feel welcome and provided some measure of assistance, the Turkish economy was in a bad state, with heavy unemployment and rampant inflation. They asked their uncle the carpet merchant to send another ten thousand dollars, and began laying plans for Europe. Unable to obtain a visa, however, they lingered in Istanbul for seven months. Their money was running out. Losing hope, Gülnar began clamoring for them to return to the Uyghur region. Mirshat, though, pointed out that both of them would surely land in prison if they returned at this point. Gülnar was persuaded. Also, she was pregnant.

Having learned from acquaintances of a sea route to Greece, Mirshat and Gülnar left Istanbul for the town of Çeşme in İzmir Province. From the Çeşme coast, one could see the lights of a Greek island. They paid twelve hundred dollars to some refugee smugglers and waited in Çeşme for a few days. Then, one night, the smugglers sent them and nearly twenty other refugees—men, women, and children—off on a worn-out little motorboat built for four or five. In the darkness, they set their course for the lights on the opposite shore. The boat was steered by one of the refugees whom the smugglers had let practice a bit during the day. After two hours on the waves, they reached the opposite shore, over-joyed at having arrived safely in Greece.

No sooner had they set foot on the shore than they found themselves surrounded by Turkish gendarmes. On the nighttime sea, with lights visible in practically all directions, they had lost their way and landed back on the Turkish coast.

The gendarmes asked the refugees one by one where they were from. When they heard that Gülnar and Mirshat were Uyghurs, they immediately contacted their captain to inform him that there were two Turks among the refugees, and that one of them was pregnant. The captain arrived at once, along with an ambulance he had called. He treated Mirshat and Gülnar as family, treating them to rotisserie kebab and bringing Gülnar to the doctor for a free checkup. They learned that the mother and baby were in good health and that she was carrying a boy.

The captain urged them not to leave for Europe, and instead to stay in Turkey and study at a university. After taking them to the immigration office to register and have their fingerprints taken, he released them. When Mirshat told him they had no Turkish residence permits, he replied, "Your being Uyghur is a residence permit. Turkey is the home-land of the Turks. No one will exclude you here. If you walk into the immigration office and apply, I'm sure they will give you a residence permit. If you run into any trouble, come find me." He handed Mirshat his business card.

They returned to Istanbul. Gülnar's belly was growing and their funds were dwindling. As they had recently arrived and did not speak Turkish well, they needed introductions from more established members of the Uyghur community to find work. At the time, though, fear of China was strong in Turkey's Uyghur community, leading to omni-present paranoia and a readiness to suspect any recent arrival of being a Chinese spy. When they asked for help from other Uyghurs in Istanbul, Mirshat and Gülnar were shut out. They decided to risk trying for Europe again.

Gülnar and Mirshat went back to İzmir. For a few months, they kept an eye on the situation and waited for another opportunity to make a run for Greece. They were embarrassed to ask their uncle again for money, but they were broke, so they asked another relative in Urumchi to send funds.

Finally, they decided to pay another smuggler to get them from Çeşme to Greece by the same sea route. The smuggler taught Mirshat a bit about steering a boat. One night when the weather was clear, Mirshat and Gülnar joined half a dozen Uzbek refugee families from Afghani-stan, young children in tow, and crowded onto another small fishing boat. Once more, they headed for that Greek island.

After they'd been on the water for an hour or so, the weather sud-

denly shifted. It began raining heavily, and the waves grew massive.
The people on the boat wailed as if it were Judgment Day. Mirshat and
Gülnar said Quran verses under their breath, asking God for protec-
tion. Gülnar was seven months pregnant.

With well over a dozen people crammed together on a boat meant for
four or five, the vessel was badly overloaded, and a wave hitting square
against the ship would have overturned the boat. Amid the rain and the
dark, everyone would have drowned. Such tragedies were common-
place in these straits. The refugees bailed rainwater out of the boat with
everything that could carry water: bottles, plastic bags, shoes, hats,
hands.

They were fortunate. With tremendous difficulty, they finally reached
the shore of the Greek island. Mirshat and Gülnar found a park, lay
down on a bench, and slept for a little while. Then they took a ferry to
Athens.

When they disembarked, they stood there for a bit, unsure of what to
do or where to go. They boarded a train for the city center. Downtown,
they saw numerous Afghan and Pakistani migrants selling cheap Chinese goods to travelers. Asking around, Mirshat was directed to an Afghan congregational mosque. Nearby were stores run by Afghans,
Pakistanis, and Chinese, as well as all manner of restaurants.

Gülnar's belly was getting big. An Uzbek youth from Afghanistan
directed them to a local hospital, and Gülnar decided she would give
birth there. They walked into a local police station, registered themselves, and received their documents. The Uzbek language is quite close
to Uyghur, and at the Afghan youth's suggestion, Gülnar and Mirshat

began working as translators between Uzbek and Chinese merchants. They made a fair bit of money, and their living circumstances improved.

The Greek economy, though, was struggling. Seeing the difficulty other migrants had in finding employment, Mirshat and Gülnar decided to keep heading north. Acquaintances in Sweden urged the couple to join them. In the meantime, Gülnar's baby was due. She gave birth in the Athens hospital the Uzbek youth had recommended.

The 2004 European Football Championship began in June. The Greek team's performance was impressive, and on July 4, Greece played Portugal for the title. As the Greek border control officers downed their beers, riveted by the televised match, Mirshat and Gülnar seized the moment. Flashing their fake visas to the distracted officers, they boarded a boat bound for Italy.

Arriving in Italy, they headed north. Crossing through Germany and Denmark, they arrived in Sweden, and there, at last, they settled. Only then did they feel safe.

When they had applied for Kazakhstani visas, they had said they were Kazakhs. Crossing illegally from Iran into Turkey, they had dressed as Kurds. In Turkey, they had introduced themselves as Uyghur Turks, and had become Turkish. When people in Greece asked where they were from, they replied that they were Korean tourists. In Athens, they had registered as Afghan refugees of Uzbek ethnicity. Only on arriving in Sweden did they feel secure in registering with their own identity. They were Uyghurs.

As we listened to their story, our mood changed with the events they recounted. At times we were wreathed in smiles; other times we were crestfallen. Not long after the story began, Gülnar and Marhaba started crying. In the patriarchal Uyghur society, it is considered shameful for men to cry, and one rarely sees such a thing. But as the story continued, Mirshat and I couldn't help ourselves. Their ten-year-old son apparently found our tears quite amusing; he had a good laugh watching the two of us. He was still a kid, and didn't yet understand the meaning of his parents' life-or-death struggles in search of freedom. He didn't know it was a miracle that he had been born safely in Athens.

After Mirshat and Gülnar arrived in Sweden, they learned Swedish fluently and trained in new professions. They now have full-time jobs in a state-run service center. They had another child, a girl. Their life now is peaceful, their family a happy one. "Our only sorrow now is that we miss our homeland," Gülnar told us.

It was our last day together. None of us wanted to say goodbye. By the time they set out with us for our hotel, it was already dark. We found a nearby metro station, consulted a map, and took the metro in the direction of our hotel. After five stops, though, we realized we had taken the wrong train. As our two families stood in the station, studying the map and discussing which direction we should head in, a Turkish man in his mid-thirties greeted us. Turkish and Uyghur being similar, the man had understood some of what we were saying. We explained the situation to him, and he told us we had been heading the wrong way just now. Our destination was in the same direction as his, he said; we should go together.

We chatted with him as we rode. Having spent several months in

Turkey, Mirshat and Gülnar were able to converse with him fairly easily. We explained about the repression Uyghurs face in China. He had
been born and raised in Paris, where he worked in construction; he told
us about the discrimination Turks face in France. If Erdoğan remained
in power, he said, he planned to immigrate to Turkey.

His own stop was a couple of stations before ours, but in the spirit of
brotherliness he stayed on till our stop. When we parted, he gave me the
prayer beads he had been handling since we met him. I was rather
moved, though I had nothing to give him in return. We embraced and
said goodbye to each other. As we were leaving the metro station, I realized I had never even asked his name.

It was midnight when we finally found the hotel. We stood in front
of the entrance and hugged Mirshat and Gülnar goodbye.

The next evening, our plane touched down in Istanbul. Uyghurs, as
a Turkic people, have an affinity for Turkey, and the chance to see Istanbul during our travels was something special for us. Over the course
of a couple of days, we walked around the city and visited various tourist sites. A Uyghur friend of mine who lived in another Turkish city
came to see us. While Marhaba continued exploring downtown, my
friend and I sat on the beach and discussed the situation back home at
length. He helped me purchase a bağlama, a seven-stringed instrument
popular in Turkey. A musician friend of mine in Urumchi had asked me
to bring one back.

On Friday evening, we boarded our flight back to Urumchi. Arriving at noon the next day, I picked up the bağlama from the flight atten-

dant and strapped it to my shoulder for safekeeping as I walked through the airport.

When we passed through border control, the same issue arose as the previous time. When my turn came, the middle-aged Han officer asked for my passport and ID card. Inspecting my ID, she asked why I had a Beijing ID number. I once again explained patiently.

She glanced at the instrument on my shoulder. "Did you study music in Beijing?"

"Yes," I replied without hesitation, lying.

Pleased with her own cleverness, she stamped my passport with gusto and sent me through. With that, we had safely crossed the border.

Not long after we returned to Urumchi, I had dinner with several friends. Fresh from my travels, I regaled them with my impressions of Europe. Suddenly, Perhat Tursun spoke up. "Can't we talk about something else? It stings every time I hear people talk about traveling abroad, like I'm hearing a conversation about a woman I was in love with but couldn't marry." Everyone cracked up. "You should get a passport, too," I told him. "When you have the chance you can go travel." His face grew gloomy. "The government won't let me leave," he said. We all fell silent.

Lost in Paris

Like a stone gate standing motionless carved with

names I stared at the sky of an unknown street

while around me the city frothed and dizzied me

drenched me in cold sweat and rain

and before I really knew her I seemed to be lost

I was truly lost

I knew

At night there was no use setting my sights by the selfless

Eiffel Tower that bravely reached down into the Seine

to fish its fate out of the murky water

so in the smelly old metro as the

iron door handle wore away like time

I watched

The road map's knotted strings seemed jumbled

like the manners of that uncouth old émigré and the heirloom

prayer beads given me by an unknown Turk aged thirty-eight

were of no use clicking softly in my pocket as

I listened

I passed two tipsy Arab shopkeepers a Latin

American taxi driver a guy delivering pizza someone walking

a dog and none of them were lost together with me

I felt

Moreover new destinations and also history romance perfume

   artwork beauties daydreams et cetera

I must forgo them all

I understood

Paris whispered to me oh you ill-starred one

go back the way you came

TWELVE

White Slips and Blue Slips

After returning from Europe, we followed Li Yang's advice and waited a full year before applying again for American visas.

In late July 2016, Marhaba, Aséna, and I took a flight to Beijing. Having turned fourteen at the end of the previous year, Aséna now had to apply for her visa in person and have her fingerprints taken at the American embassy.

Arriving at Beijing Capital International Airport, we hailed a cab to the Xinjiang Affairs Complex. It was almost one a.m. when we arrived.

There were no free rooms at the hotel we had stayed at during our last visit. It was tourist season, and demand was high; one had to book in advance. It was an oversight on my part.

We walked over to another hotel in the Xinjiang Affairs Complex courtyard. Its doors were already locked for the night. Farther along, the lobby of the upscale Xinjiang Suites was open, but the lights had been extinguished. The lone guard sat in a corner fiddling with his phone. As soon as he saw us enter, he waved his hand to indicate there were no free rooms.

Lugging our suitcases out of the courtyard, we flagged down a taxi and headed to Weigongcun Street, alongside Nationalities University. There wasn't a soul in sight. With our suitcases clattering behind us, the three of us wandered like ghosts in search of a hotel. A few small inns were open, but at each one, before we could finish asking about vacancies, the staff saw that we were Uyghur and answered with a curt "No."

Our options exhausted, we took a cab back to the Xinjiang Affairs Complex. Returning to the first hotel, we inquired once more about vacancies in the foolish hope that a room might have opened up. The concierge told us some rooms would be available at daybreak.

There was nothing to do now but sit on the stone bench under the copse of trees in front of the building and wait for morning. Setting our suitcases next to us, we sank onto the bench. It was the most humid time of the year in Beijing. The city's wily mosquitos, so familiar to me from my student days, were hungry. The incessant singing of the cicadas wore on our nerves.

Marhaba and Aséna, never having encountered this kind of humidity, groaned that it was like a greenhouse. Marhaba was breathing heavily. Mosquitoes had always been fond of Aséna, and she grew irritated as she sat there fending them off. On top of that, my stomach was growling with hunger, and I could tell how hungry Marhaba and Aséna were, too. Again and again, I tried to offer words of comfort, but everything I said echoed strangely in my ears. My sleepless head was heavy from exhaustion, discomfort, and the humidity. I hoped no one would see us in this wretched state.

"Tahir Hamut," Marhaba said bitterly, "if they don't give us a visa this time, don't mention the word 'America' in front of me again!"

In the morning we checked into a hotel room and slept until noon. The next day we went to the American embassy. As agreed, Li Yang met us there in front of the complex.

The line was even longer than last time. After shuffling through the queue for more than two hours, we had our fingerprints taken, and finally we were once more in that corridor with visa officials.

"Maybe this time we'll get a male official," whispered Marhaba. "Why do you say that?" asked Aséna. "Women are mean," Marhaba replied. I chuckled.

Despite Marhaba's wishes, we were directed to a female visa official's window. She was pretty and blond, like the official we had met last time, but younger.

I handed her our four passports. I held the rest of our materials at the ready in case she requested them.

"Why are you planning to go to America?" she asked in excellent Chinese.

"A family trip," I responded calmly.

From the four passports, the woman selected mine and checked its contents against her computer records. She put the passport down and typed something into the computer. Then she picked up my passport again and opened it to the page with the Italian visa. She took a pen-shaped device from a lanyard around her neck and pressed it to the visa;

the device emitted a blue light. She must be verifying that the visa is authentic, I thought.

The woman put the passport down. "Is your company based in Urumchi?" she asked. "It is," I replied. "Do you live in Urumchi?" I told her that we did.

She typed some more on her computer. Then, not lifting her eyes from the screen, she reached across the counter for the other three passports. Excitement rose within me: this was a sign that our visa applications would be approved. If a visa was granted, the passport would be retained, stamped with the visa, and returned to its owner by post.

Moments later, she looked up at us and smiled. "Congratulations! You've been issued American tourist visas." With a swift motion of her hands, she held out two blue slips of paper. I breathed a deep, silent sigh of relief. Aséna squirmed with happiness. Marhaba's face opened like a flower. After expressing our heartfelt gratitude to the visa official, we headed outside. None of the materials we had brought turned out to be needed.

"Let me have those," said Aséna, taking the blue slips from my hand as we walked out of the building. "I want to show them off as we walk by!"

As we passed by the line of people waiting to enter the embassy, Aséna, true to her word, clutched the blue slips high and proud for all to see.

On leaving the embassy, the first thing I did was send a voice message to my friend Jüret in America to share the good news. "Attaboy!" he replied excitedly. Li Yang also warmly congratulated us.

We hailed a taxi back to the hotel. "Dad," said Aséna, "while that visa official was checking our passports, I could hear your heart pounding."

A month after we received our American visas, Chen Quanguo was appointed party secretary of the Uyghur Autonomous Region. Uyghur intellectuals took immediate note of the fact that Chen had previously been party secretary of Tibet, where he had cracked down hard on Tibetan dissent. Surmising that such an official would bring only harsh policies to the Uyghur region, our unease grew deeper still.

Now that we had our visas, Jüret began urging us to hurry. We still hadn't made up our minds, though, about immigrating to America. Jüret insisted that if we had the chance, we should at least come and see the United States. I called Li Yang, who told me that plane tickets were relatively cheap now that tourist season was over. Marhaba and I decided to take a fifteen-day trip.

We consulted with Jüret before purchasing our tickets; we would spend most of our trip at his home in northern Virginia. Then I wrote my friend Kamil, who was at Indiana University as a visiting scholar. He was delighted when he heard we would be in the United States, and we started making plans to meet in Indiana. At the time, the American ethnomusicologist Elise Anderson was also at Indiana University, where she was finishing her doctorate. Beginning in 2012, she had spent around three years in our homeland researching Uyghur music. We had been on friendly terms during her time there, and when she heard we were coming to Indiana she invited me to hold a poetry reading at her university. I happily agreed.

It didn't take long to prepare for the journey. With the dining challenges of our Europe trip still fresh in our memory, we packed two boxes of naan for the road. For Uyghurs, this flatbread is not merely a food; it has rich symbolic meaning. Newlyweds take bites out of a naan dipped in salt water. People sometimes invoke naan when taking an oath. Naan must not be laid upside down, nor may it be stepped on. When visiting someone, naan is a valued gift. Elders say that "on a journey, naan is a companion," and advise taking naan wherever one travels. We figured halal food might be hard to find in America; and if not, we knew that our Uyghur friends in the United States would be missing naan from their homeland.

In mid-September we flew to Beijing. Following a night at the Xinjiang Affairs Complex hotel, we returned in the morning to Beijing Capital International Airport and passed smoothly through border control. After an eighteen-hour flight, we arrived at Dulles International Airport in Washington, DC. At customs, an officer pointed to the two boxes of naan.

"What's in there?"

"Food," I replied. It was one of the relatively few English words I knew.

"What kind of food?" he asked.

I didn't know how to explain. Fortunately, immediately after asking his question he continued the conversation he was having with another officer, thereby giving me a chance to think. Intending to convey that naan was made from wheat, I stood there trying to remember the English word for wheat.

Marhaba walked up to me. "What did he say?"

"He asked me what was in the box," I replied with frustration.

"Why don't you just tell him it's naan?" she said, raising her voice a bit.

As soon as he heard the word "naan," the customs officer waved us on through. He turned back to his colleague to continue their conversation. I was surprised and delighted that the customs officer knew what naan was. We walked out of customs and saw Jüret and his wife. They had been waiting anxiously, worried that the delay might mean something had happened to us.

Embracing them, we told them what had just transpired at customs. They replied that practically everyone in America knew what naan was, and that it was eaten not only by Uyghurs but also by numerous communities in Central Asia, South Asia, and the Middle East.

Numerous Uyghurs had settled in the DC suburbs in northern Virginia, making it the largest Uyghur community in America. From what I could tell, there were two reasons for this. First, as the capital city, Washington was where Uyghurs could pursue their political advocacy, and most Uyghur activists therefore lived in the area. Second, there was Radio Free Asia. Founded to provide unfiltered news to people in countries where speech was restricted, in the late 1990s the station began broadcasting a Uyghur-language news service that was widely followed in our homeland. A number of DC Uyghurs worked at this Uyghur news service. While the Uyghur community in the Washington area had grown up around the radio employees and the political activists, by now the community numbered four or five thousand, with people engaged in all kinds of professions.

For the Chinese government, then, northern Virginia was "a nest of splittists," home to numerous advocates of Uyghur independence. Uyghurs visiting Washington as tourists were warned by the Chinese authorities not to mix with DC Uyghurs and not to visit the areas where they lived. Tour companies also took care on this point.

For this reason, during our fifteen days in the United States, we met only with a few families we were particularly close to. Needless to say, we were forced to be discreet even about these meetings. The friends we met with included activists for Uyghur freedom as well as several employees of Radio Free Asia, which the Chinese government considered "enemy radio." Even more problematic was that Uyghurs here suspected certain members of their community of being spies sent by the Chinese government. If this was true, we had to be careful, or else China's national security organs would know whom we had met with before we even returned to Urumchi.

We spoke at great length, though, with those friends we did see. Most of those we visited had not returned to the Uyghur region since coming to America; they missed their homeland and were anxious to know how relatives and friends were doing. With the situation back home deteriorating by the day, we had little good news to offer them. Our conversations would begin with excitement and end with deep sighs.

Jüret was a board member at the Uyghur American Association, and one day he invited the association's president, Ilshat Hassan, to his home to meet with me. Ilshat and I spoke at length about the circumstances Uyghurs faced, about the state of affairs for intellectuals in our homeland, and about Ilham Tohti in particular. Jüret told Ilshat that we were considering immigrating to the United States. As we were saying our goodbyes, Ilshat turned to me. "It would be best if you didn't come to America." I didn't ask him why he said this, and he left without explaining further. I took him to mean that a Uyghur intellectual like me could do more for our people by remaining in our homeland. I still think sometimes of the contemplative look on Ilshat Hassan's face when he said this to me.

A few days later, when we arrived at Indiana University, Kamil came out to welcome us. My old friend and I embraced. Kamil's wife, Munire, was still in Urumchi, and Kamil's nine-year-old daughter, Tumaris, was as happy to see Marhaba as if she were seeing her own mother.

The poetry reading was held in an auditorium on the first floor of a class building and was open to the public. A large screen on the wall displayed my photo and the event title "Summer Is a Conspiracy," taken from one of my poems. Twenty or thirty people were in attendance, most of them students.

After Elise Anderson briefly introduced me, we began the program of eight poems in Uyghur and English. For the first poem, I recited "Summer Is a Conspiracy." As Elise began reading the English translation, I looked out over the students listening carefully to the verses. I had written the poem during my own student years, and was now flooded with recollections of those times: so full of hope, heady emotion, and zest for life. Never in those days did I imagine I would one day recite my poems at an American university.

After we returned from Indiana, Jüret took us to several shopping centers. We wandered through the stores, looking at prices. Given that Jüret had been constantly urging us to immigrate to the United States, we figured we should get a sense of conditions here. We asked around about how Uyghurs supported themselves in America, and about the cost of housing and goods.

While shopping in DC, Marhaba busied herself converting the prices to Chinese renminbi. I teased her for spending time on something so pointless, but she somehow managed to bargain on prices without knowing a word of English. She didn't waste time wondering whether it was appropriate to haggle over prices in a country we barely knew. Back home, her merciless bargaining often made me sweat, and I would edge away in discomfort. When I told her it was unseemly to haggle so fiercely, she would counter, "Was it easy for us to make this money?" While these were two different issues, in truth her frugal and fastidious homemaking had helped ensure our family's economic stability. She always worked to find inexpensive, high-quality items, and would constantly compare prices in different stores. She considered this worth the time and inconvenience, and her ability to remember prices amazed me. For Marhaba, this was a way to challenge herself and a source of pride. She made sure that our daughters followed her example as well: they, too, purchased things with care, never wasting money.

If we were to start life anew in an unknown country, living frugally would assume a still greater importance. Observing Marhaba's skill at home economy, one of our friends declared with conviction: "If you come to America, seems like you'll make it." For a family still hesitant about the prospect of moving abroad, these simple words meant a great deal.

THIRTEEN

Into the Storm

While we returned from our trip to the United States with very fond memories, we were not yet ready to leave everything and move abroad. Over the next half-year, though, as the Chinese state's growing repression in our homeland culminated in mass arrests of Uyghurs, we came to see things differently. Following our chilling experience in the police station basement, we began making discreet preparations to leave the country. We had Li Yang purchase plane tickets to the United States and exchanged some of our renminbi for dollars on the black market. Now we had to wait several weeks for our daughters' summer vacation to begin, in order to lend credence to our story of a family tour of the US. We just had to hope we could make it to summer without a problem.

In mid-June 2017, the Urumchi weather grew hot. If there was something I needed to do at the office, I tried to go in the afternoon after it cooled down a little. One day, following an afternoon at the office, I drove home around six.

As I did every day, I turned off Unity Road and took the outer ring road to Zhongquan Street, turning after a while onto Nanwan. As I drove along, lost in thought, I noticed traffic beginning to slow. Wondering what was happening, I opened the window and craned my neck to look ahead.

On the left side of the road, military police officers were dismounting from open-topped transports. Each one carried an automatic weapon.

At that moment, three police sedans pulled up behind the transport trucks. The officers who emerged from these cars began directing the military police units, dividing them into groups and assigning them to alleyways. Beside them were seven or eight neighborhood committee officials with blue ID badges around their necks and blue clipboards in their hands.

The air was thick with tension. Scenes we had previously seen only in the movies were now part of everyday life.

With a single shouted order, the military police raced down the alleys. They were heading to the small, plain houses along those streets to arrest the Uyghurs who lived there or search their homes.

As a Han-majority city, and as a regional capital that received some global attention, Urumchi had always been governed less strictly than other parts of our homeland, and we lived there relatively comfortably. Now, though, our life in the capital had begun to change in ways we had never imagined. The frightening rumors we had heard over the last few months were becoming our reality.

...

For the past month, work had come to a halt at my company. Barely leaving the apartment, I hadn't done much besides eat and sleep, and had begun to feel like a lamb being fattened for slaughter. The constant anxiety weighed on me, and each day my body and spirit hung heavier.

I found myself unable to work. I didn't even have the concentration to watch television or read. The thought of writing poetry seemed laughable. My wife and daughters and I couldn't find much to say. Going out for a walk in the evening offered a little relief.

"Don't stay out too long or I'll get worried," Marhaba reminded me, as she did every day. She feared I would be detained on the street and taken away.

I walked along the big street in front of our apartment complex. The roads were crimson with the sunset.

While I left the house each evening hoping my walk would bring me some peace, I invariably found myself thinking about everything unfolding in the city. Innumerable people had been summoned back to their hometowns or sent to the camps. In this capital city, where Uyghurs had always been a minority, they were now even fewer. Those remaining were caught up in fear and turmoil.

I kept walking. The old city's Uyghur neighborhoods were deserted.

I ran into a man I knew named Polat, a Kashgari like myself. He had also come out for a walk after dinner. We exchanged pleasantries and walked together, and I told him what I had seen that day at Nanwan

Street. As we continued walking, he told me something that had happened in his old neighborhood in Kashgar.

In May, the government had required all Uyghurs in Kashgar to hand over any religious items in their homes. Frightened by the ongoing roundups, most people surrendered all belongings relating to their faith: religious books, prayer rugs, prayer beads, even articles of clothing. Some devout individuals were unwilling to part with their Qurans, but with neighbors and even relatives betraying each other, those who kept their Qurans were quickly found, detained, and harshly punished. Recently in Polat's neighborhood, a man in his seventies had come across a Quran in his house that he hadn't been able to find following the previous month's confiscation order. The old man was afraid that if he turned it over now to neighborhood officials, they would ask why he hadn't relinquished it earlier, accuse him of incorrect thinking, and take him away to be punished, so he wrapped the Quran in a plastic bag and threw it in the Tuman River. For safety purposes, though, wire mesh had been installed under all bridges over the Tuman. When the mesh was cleaned, the Quran was found and turned over to the authorities. Inside the Quran, the police found a copy of the old man's ID card. Elderly people had a habit of keeping important documents in frequently read books, so that they could find them when needed. The police quickly tracked down the old man and detained him on charges of engaging in illegal religious activities. Just recently, they had sentenced him to seven years in prison.

While relating all of this, Polat repeatedly checked our surroundings. If anyone was approaching us on the sidewalk, he would stop speaking immediately.

Such stories were common now among Uyghurs. We told them to each other in whispers.

Around that time, Marhaba and I decided to visit her cousin. We drove over to her apartment complex at the northeast edge of the city.

After the 2009 violence in Urumchi, the Chinese government had implemented a policy it called the Slum Renovation Project, which entailed the wholesale demolition of houses in the old city's predominantly Uyghur districts. Many of the Uyghurs whose homes were demolished were provided cheap apartments constructed on the city's outskirts.

Marhaba's cousin had moved to this complex in 2010. Although the apartments in the complex were shoddy at best, the demolished neighborhoods' former residents, their livelihoods now ruined, were thankful to have somewhere to live.

Marhaba's cousin lived with her son in a one-bedroom apartment on the sixth floor. She and her husband had divorced three years before. Her son, Arman, had graduated from college two years earlier with a degree in highway engineering. Like many Uyghur college graduates, he was unable to find a position in his field, and since college had been working odd jobs.

After dinner, Arman told us what had happened in the complex over the past five days. On Monday, the neighborhood committee and the police had delivered an urgent joint order at the morning flag-raising ceremony, which all residents—like the residents of every neighborhood in Xinjiang—were required to attend daily. The order stated that each household must turn over all Islamic items to neighborhood committee officials within three days; those who failed to do so would be responsible for the consequences. The neighborhood was thrown into a panic, and many people brought their Qurans and other religious items to the neighborhood committee office. Some people worried it would be a sin to turn these items over for the state to burn, and they hid their books and prayer rugs in their homes. Rumors began circulating, though, that the police had a special device that could detect hidden religious objects. The people who had hidden Islamic items grew terrified. The previous night, as soon as it grew dark, they began furtively tossing their religious articles down the manholes that led to the complex's sewer system. To avoid tripping over each other, they hid in the buildings; when one person returned from tossing out their items, the next would run out, throw their items into the manhole, and run back inside. All of this happened quickly and surreptitiously, but because there were many people with items to throw out, it continued throughout the night. Some people sprinted out the door and stumbled into others, after which both would retreat to the building. Arman watched all this from his window, chuckling to himself. When dawn broke, people found some sacred items simply discarded in front of the building. Later that morning, neighborhood committee officials and police officers came to make the rounds of the complex. They asked some people what had happened. Later, they collected all the discarded items from the storm drains, loaded them onto a truck, and drove them away.

The confiscation of household religious items, particularly Qurans and other Islamic books, was gathering strength throughout Urumchi. Marhaba and I discussed what to do with the religious books in our home.

In our apartment, we had three copies of the Quran, one each in Uyghur, Arabic, and Chinese, as well as Uyghur-language editions of a few other common books relating to Islam. None of these were prohibited books; all had been published with state sanction. Recently, though, many previously legal things had become illegal. It was impossible to say what was permitted and what was not; what counted was whatever the government said at any given moment. The government, for us, meant the neighborhood committee officials, the officers at the local police station, or the officers of the state security organs.

"Keep these books with your other books," suggested Marhaba. "Since you're a writer, they shouldn't object if you say you kept the books for professional use."

"If I say that, you seriously think they'll believe me?"

She paused a moment. "Or maybe we should hide the books?"

"And if they search the house and find them?"

"What should we do, then?"

Finally, we decided to bring the half-dozen books, along with our three prayer mats, to her aunt and uncle's house. Not wanting to risk discussing it over the phone, we simply told them we were coming for a visit. Before we left our apartment, we checked each of the books thoroughly.

At their house, we explained the situation. "Good thinking. We'll keep the books here," said Marhaba's aunt. "We are old," added her uncle. "I doubt the authorities will bother with us. They know we're not a threat." We felt relieved.

A few days later, we were home eating lunch when my cousin Mustafa called from Kashgar. My heart skipped a beat. Mustafa never called unless there was something important. These days, with bad news arriving from all quarters, I worried constantly about my family in Kashgar. I wasn't surprised, then, when Mustafa began the conversation by asking if I knew where the women's prison was located in Ghulja. He had thought we might know, given that Ghulja is Marhaba's hometown. I asked him what the matter was.

A month ago, his mother-in-law, a woman in her sixties, had been arrested. Six years earlier, one of her neighbors had held a Quran reading for the women in the neighborhood. Because Mustafa's mother-in-law was a bit unwell, she arrived late at the gathering. The Quran recitation had already begun and the room was completely filled with women, so Mustafa's mother-in-law sat on her haunches on the concrete doorstep. Before long, her legs grew uncomfortable and she headed home.

This April, as the mass arrests gathered steam, those in their apartment complex who had not yet been detained were forced to assemble each evening in a large hall to study the party's policies. At these sessions, people were pressured by the authorities to denounce each other. For her crime of sitting for five minutes on that doorstep six years earlier, his mother-in-law had been denounced and arrested.

Yesterday, her family heard she had been sentenced to five years and sent to the Ghulja women's prison. This information hadn't been received through official government channels, though, but rather through asking around over the previous month, and it needed to be confirmed. Her family hoped at the very least to find her, visit her, and bring her necessary items and medical supplies.

Unfortunately, we didn't know anything about the Ghulja women's prison. I told Mustafa I was sorry we couldn't help him, and said goodbye.

Marhaba's aunt called me one evening toward the end of June. After we briefly exchanged greetings, she told me why she had called. "There's a storm brewing in our neighborhood, so I sorted those things out."

Her voice was strained. I knew what storm she was referring to: the house searches must have reached her neighborhood. After many years of political repression, Uyghurs were accustomed to using coded language. A political campaign was a "storm," while innocent people caught up in mass arrests or in a Strike Hard Campaign were said to be "gone with the wind." A "guest" at home often meant a state security agent. If someone had been arrested, they were "in the hospital"; the number of days they were to be in treatment marked the years of a prison sentence.

"Which things did you sort out?" I asked Marhaba's aunt.

She lowered her voice. "Those things you brought over the other day."

We visited them frequently, and in accordance with Uyghur custom we usually brought food or gifts. With all the recent chaos, it took me a moment to catch her meaning. "Which things we brought over? Just tell me."

"Those books! The books!" she said with frustration, lowering her voice still further despite her bitter tone.

"How did you sort them out?" I couldn't keep the dismay out of my voice.

"Don't ask," she replied. "We took care of it."

I found myself imagining all the different ways the books might have been dealt with. Did they burn them, throw them out, or perhaps hide them? Unable to get it off my mind, I found my thoughts drifting toward my friend Kamil, who years earlier had run into trouble because of a book.

FOURTEEN

Waiting to Be Arrested at Night

At noon on the last day of June, Marhaba and I sat in the living room listlessly discussing what to have for lunch. Our spirits were low, the air was stuffy, and no food sounded appealing. Finally we decided not to make lunch, and instead just to have milk tea with naan and salad. We silently began preparing the food.

Marhaba spoke suddenly. "It's been a week since I've heard from Munire. I leave voice messages for her on WeChat and she doesn't get back to me. You don't think something's happened to them, do you?" I felt a bit anxious when I heard this. Munire and her husband, Kamil, were dear friends of ours.

Mass arrests of Uyghurs had been underway for two months in Urumchi. Fear was everywhere. For that reason, we had been meeting up with or messaging our close friends and family on a regular basis. Although we couldn't protect anyone from the arrests, it gave us some measure of comfort to hear from each other frequently.

Munire and Marhaba spoke almost every day. It was unusual for Munire to be silent this long.

"Leave her another message," I said. "Maybe she'll respond."

Marhaba picked up her phone. "Salam, Munire, how have you been? I've sent you a few messages and haven't heard back—we're a bit worried. If you're there, please say something."

Not long after, a voice message arrived from Munire.

"How are you doing, Marhaba? I'm here." Munire's voice was despondent.

"How's Kamil? Tahir is asking after him."

"Kamil's not here."

"What happened to Kamil?" Marhaba asked. "He hasn't gone away, has he?"

"Let it go for now, my friend, I'm feeling under the weather. Let's talk later."

Kamil and I had studied together at Kashgar Uyghur High School, then in Beijing at the Central University for Nationalities . In Beijing we grew close as we shared ideas and experiences. Kamil was an even-tempered, earnest, and hardworking young man. His interests ran to linguistics and philosophy. When I graduated in 1992 I stayed in Beijing to work; Kamil graduated the next year and returned to Urumchi, where he took a position at a research institute. Before long, I also returned to Urumchi, and we saw each other frequently. Around that time, Kamil met Munire; after a while, they got married. They'd always been happy together.

In February 2016, Kamil received a stipend from China's Ministry of

Education to spend a year at Indiana University as a visiting scholar. His daughter, Tumaris, went with him and attended school there. Munire visited them in Indiana for more than a month. While they were in America, some of their friends in the United States urged them not to go back, given the worsening political situation in the Uyghur region. When Marhaba and I visited Indiana University, we discussed the matter with Kamil. I also felt that their best option was to remain in the US, but Marhaba remained silent.

The choice was anything but simple. Before Kamil left for the United States, the Chinese government had required that two of his friends serve as guarantors; if Kamil did not return, they would be punished. Kamil did not want to stay in America at the price of a lifetime's guilty conscience. In addition, if Kamil's family remained in the United States, the Chinese government would seize their apartment in Urumchi and cut off their salaries. It would take a year or so for them to achieve US residency and receive permission to work and support themselves. Their family's finances during that year would inevitably be strained.

Kamil was a very cautious intellectual. His family finally decided not to stay in America. Kamil's year abroad ended, and in February 2017 he and his daughter returned to Urumchi. The mass internments of Uyghurs began the following month.

In May, Kamil's family and our family went to Turpan together. The two-day trip passed pleasantly, particularly for our daughters. Tumaris had missed her homeland during the year she spent in the United States, and Aséna and Almila enjoyed spending time with her.

While we were in Turpan, Kamil and I were eating apricots in an orchard and we started talking. He suddenly told me he was worried he would be detained during the ongoing mass arrests. I asked him why. In fall 2013, he told me, he had attended an academic conference in Turkey at the invitation of the Turkish organization Silk Road Society and the cultural NGO Turkish Hearths. It was Kamil's first trip abroad. Recently, he had learned that Turkish Hearths had been blacklisted by the Chinese government as a "foreign splittist organization." Even though Kamil had attended the conference only after completing the appropriate paperwork and obtaining permission from his research institute and the police department, many things that had once been permitted were now becoming unacceptable, even criminal.

In September 2014, Kamil had joined nearly a hundred Chinese citizens taking part in a monthlong exchange program in the United States under the auspices of the State Department's prestigious International Visitor Leadership Program. This time, too, on the basis of his invitation from the US embassy in China, Kamil had received permission from his workplace and the government's foreign affairs organs. Even so, officers from the Autonomous Region Bureau of State Security had met with Kamil before he left for America and after he returned to Urumchi. Then, too, Kamil had lived in fear for a time.

As we were leaving the apricot orchard, Kamil spoke to me in a low voice. "Before my most recent trip to the US, and again after I returned, state security officers came to speak with me just like they did last time. At their request, I told them everything that happened while I was in the US. I don't think it will cause me any problems. There's nothing else to be concerned about there." Then he added glumly, "But I'm still worrying about that Turkish conference."

Kamil didn't know whether he should regret his decision not to stay in America, but there was no going back now. By the terms of the American and Chinese governments' agreement, after visiting scholars in the United States returned to China, they could not reenter America for two years. In addition, as soon as Kamil returned from the US, his workplace had confiscated his passport. By that time, the passports of all Uyghurs working in government offices had already been taken away.

For these reasons and perhaps also for others we didn't know, Kamil and Munire had quarreled frequently since his return. Some time ago, when Marhaba and I had gone by their apartment for a visit, America came up in conversation, and with a few cutting remarks they had begun arguing bitterly right in front of us. Now, after Marhaba's WeChat exchange with Munire, we thought something similar must have happened. We decided to visit them within the next couple of days to help them settle their differences.

On Sunday morning we called Munire to tell her we'd be coming by, and that afternoon Marhaba and I drove over to their place.

Kamil's research institute was built around a compact, attractive courtyard. Like many of his colleagues, Kamil lived in one of the courtyard's apartment buildings, about a hundred meters from the building where he worked.

I stopped the car in front of Kamil's apartment building. Tumaris was playing there with some other kids. When she saw us she ran up and told us her mom was in the apartment. Then she ran back to play with her friends.

Their apartment was on the third floor. Munire opened the door. Her face was drawn, her unease palpable. She led us to the couch in the living room; we took a seat and exchanged the usual pleasantries. "Is Kamil not home?" I asked. Munire hastily put her right index finger to her lips, and with her left hand pointed to the ceiling. Her meaning was clear: we must not mention Kamil, since there might be a listening device in the apartment. Marhaba and I immediately understood the gravity of the situation.

"Let's head down to the courtyard," Munire said wearily.

We walked out of the building together. The air was humid. In the small park in front of the building, a few Uyghur women sat on a long bench, talking in the shade. Munire avoided them and led us to a bench some distance away. The moment we sat down on the bench she burst into tears. Our hearts hurt as we looked at her, not knowing what to say. After a little while, Munire dried her eyes and began telling us in a soft voice what had happened.

Around five p.m. on Monday, June 19, Munire had finished making dinner and texted Kamil at the office: "Dinner is ready."

"I'll be home in a bit," he replied. But a half hour went by with no sign of Kamil.

Munire texted him again. "The food's getting cold. Where are you?"

Now Kamil wrote back. "You guys go ahead, I'll eat later." Oddly, he was texting in Chinese, rather than their native Uyghur.

Another half hour went by. Munire was getting worried. "Are you all right? Why haven't you come home yet?"

This time Kamil didn't respond. Munire went downstairs, walked over to Kamil's office building, and looked up at the fourth-floor office where he worked. The windows were dark. Munire immediately called Kamil, but he didn't pick up. She called Ghalip, a colleague of Kamil's who worked in the same office, and asked about Kamil. Ghalip said they needed to speak in person. His apartment was in the same courtyard, and Munire walked over to his building. Ghalip came downstairs and told Munire what had happened that afternoon.

Around four o'clock, while Kamil, Ghalip, and their colleague Esqer were working in their office, Kamil received a phone call. By the end of the call, he looked ashen. He left the office in an agitated state and headed downstairs. Sensing that something was wrong, Ghalip and Esqer looked down from the office window and saw three men load Kamil into a car and drive off. Ghalip and Esqer assumed the men were state security officers.

Munire called Kamil again as soon as she returned to her apartment. No answer. She texted him, and this time he wrote back. He was fine, he said, the police just had some questions for him, and he would come home after he answered them. But after this, his texts stopped.

Two days later, three police officers drove Kamil home. One of the officers took Munire to wait in the park in front of their building while the other two officers led Kamil into their apartment. Two hours later, the officers emerged with Kamil and his laptop. They drove off. Munire returned home to find their apartment turned upside down. Closets, drawers, chests, and suitcases had been flung open. In the bedroom, even the mattress and bed frame had been dismantled and thrown to the floor. Kamil's books and papers lay scattered everywhere. The police had searched their house for two hours and in the end took only Kamil's laptop. Munire had no idea what they had been searching for.

The next day, Kamil texted her again. "They're taking me to Kashgar," he wrote in Chinese. "Please bring me a few changes of clothes." In an hour, she should come to the front gate of the Academy of Sciences courtyard, near the Autonomous Region Bureau of State Security. A police officer would come out to meet her. Munire wrote back to ask what else Kamil needed, but he didn't reply.

Munire brought the clothing. Kamil was being held in an apartment in one of the Academy of Sciences buildings. The moment he saw Munire he started crying. He couldn't bring himself to speak. The police told Munire to trust that the government would resolve the situation fairly; in the meantime, she should not inquire about Kamil. If necessary, they would get in touch with her. Then they sent her home. After that, Munire lost all contact with Kamil. She had no idea what had happened to him.

I felt cold sweat on my back. Marhaba had gone pale. We told Munire we were ready to help in any way we were able, and gave her all the words of comfort we could. But everything we said to reassure her felt utterly lifeless and futile.

Before we left, Munire asked us not to tell anyone what had happened. Usually there were two reasons for this. First, no matter the cause of an arrest, and regardless of whether it was just or unjust, people were extremely wary regarding those who had been detained. If one member of a family was arrested, especially for political reasons, those who caught wind of it would feel uneasy around that family or even avoid them. Second, in the event that the arrested person was soon released, the lid would stay on the pot and no one would know. It would be as if it had never happened. If someone was kept in detention for a while, though, it was impossible to hide. Everyone understood this. We promised Munire we would tell no one. Needless to say, we also had no desire to be the bearers of this bad news.

After we parted with Munire, we were heading toward our car when Tumaris ran up again to say goodbye to us. Seeing how happy she looked, I sensed that Munire must have kept Kamil's arrest from her. Even if Tumaris did know, perhaps she was too young to understand how terrifying it all was.

The sky was growing dark. Dusk was falling. People were hurrying home from work.

I drove home via the outer ring road. Marhaba knew how heavy a blow Kamil's arrest was for me. We were silent all the way home.

Years earlier, after I had returned from Beijing and started working as a teacher in Urumchi, Kamil told me of a six-volume set of Chinese-language books in the library of the institute where he worked. Intended for internal circulation only, the mimeographed books were entitled *Studies on Pan-Islamism and Pan-Turkism*. These books were compiled to help "purge the poison" of so-called Pan-Islamism and Pan-Turkism from the Uyghur region, and to assist in the struggle against "ethnic separatism." Two of the volumes were translations of foreign scholars' writings on the Uyghur issue. The government permitted only select researchers and officials to view such books and materials; the rest of us rarely had a chance to encounter them. I was eager to see the books, and at my request, Kamil borrowed those two volumes from the institute library for me. After I finished reading them, though, I became extremely busy with preparations for going abroad, and forgot to return them to Kamil.

Not long after, when my plans to study in Turkey ended with my arrest at a Chinese border crossing, my interrogators asked who knew that I planned to go abroad. I told them that Kamil and another friend of mine were aware of my plans. When the police searched my room at the Urumchi school where I worked, they found those two books. Kamil was now in deep trouble. As the police interrogated me over the following month, they frequently called him in for unscheduled questioning as well. Finally, after the police failed to turn up any evidence of a crime that would justify taking me to court, they ceased questioning Kamil. I was kept in custody, and later sent without trial to the labor camp.

I thought about all of this as I drove home from Kamil and Munire's apartment. Usually, if one Uyghur was arrested, the authorities would target others connected with the case as well as the arrested individual's close friends and family.

That night, after our daughters had gone to sleep, I took a pair of sturdy autumn shoes from the shoe cupboard and put them behind the door. Then I rummaged through the wardrobe in our bedroom and from my winter clothes pulled out a pair of jeans, a sweater, and a roomy coat. I put a small towel in the pocket of the coat. As I sat folding these on the bed, Marhaba finished what she was doing and came into the bedroom. She looked at me with surprise.

"What are you doing?"

"I'm preparing, just in case."

"For what?"

"They might come for me, too. If they take me away I want to be warmly dressed."

"You mean because of what happened with Kamil?"

"It might happen like that, it might happen for some other reason. I just have a feeling."

"Don't frighten yourself. Nothing's going to happen to you."

"You know perfectly well you don't believe that. These months, these days, there is nothing that can't happen to us."

I continued folding the clothes as I spoke. "You know that the other people who were in the labor camp with me twenty years ago have already been arrested again. I've never been as worried about this as I am now."

She looked sadly at the clothing. "It would be better to take that black sweater you have, it's warmer."

"It's too thick. I can't be seen wearing a thick sweater when it's practically July," I joked. I put the pile of folded clothing next to the bed.

Since the mass arrests had begun, most detained Uyghurs had been summoned by phone to the local neighborhood committee or police station and then taken away. But some, especially intellectuals, had been taken from their homes in the middle of the night. From what I had heard, after midnight the police would knock on the door of the person they planned to arrest. As soon as the person opened the door the police would confirm their name, slap handcuffs on their wrists, and haul them off. They wouldn't even let them change clothes; whatever they were wearing is what they would leave in. Some people had been taken away in their pajamas.

Everyone knew what happened next. The police would take their prisoner to a jail cell or a camp lockup, where there was nothing besides a high ceiling, four thick walls, a camera in every corner, an iron door, and a chilly cement floor. If you felt hot you could remove clothes, but if you were cold there was nothing you could do. Even in high summer this was a practical problem one had to consider. If someone knocked at my door in the middle of the night, I planned to put on these warm clothes and autumn shoes before answering. Even though Kamil was arrested during the day, I had a strong feeling they would come for me at night.

Marhaba and I were both silent for a moment. We lay side by side on the bed.

"Why do you think they arrested Kamil?" she asked.

"I've been thinking about it," I said hesitantly, "and I just can't figure it out. Kamil himself probably doesn't know."

We fell silent again. I turned out the light.

"I'm going to ask you something," I said, "and you have to promise me you'll do it."

"What is it? Tell me first."

"I'm serious," I said firmly. "Promise me first."

"All right," she replied quietly.

"If they arrest me, don't lose yourself. Don't make inquiries about me, don't go looking for help, don't spend money trying to get me out. This time isn't like any time before. They are planning something dark. There is no notifying families or inquiring at police stations this time. So don't trouble yourself with that. Keep our family affairs in order, take good care of our daughters, make sure life goes on as if I were still here. I'm not afraid of prison. I am afraid of you and the girls struggling and suffering when I'm gone. So I want you to remember what I'm saying."

"Do you have to talk like you're heading to your death?" she asked uneasily.

"You know the PIN numbers for my bank cards," I added.

Marhaba began crying. I had turned off the light so that I wouldn't see her cry. In the pitch black there was no sound but her quiet sobbing.

Throughout the next week I remained prepared for arrest. Marhaba and I called Munire three times to ask whether there was any news from Kamil. There was no news. We gradually got the impression that Munire didn't want us to keep asking, so we stopped.

A week went by without incident. I felt that the most dangerous moment had passed, and grew slightly calmer. But I kept those clothes ready beside the bed.

It turned out I was not the only one sleeping with a set of warm clothes at the ready. One evening, when I went out to buy milk at the convenience store in front of our apartment complex, I ran into a young translator I knew named Adil. Since graduating five years earlier from Xinjiang University's Uyghur Literature Department, Adil had been unable to find work in his field of study and instead made his living as a translator of Arabic and Turkish. These days, he lived in fear. Foreign connections, a history of travel abroad, and even having relatives and friends in other countries were now enough to get Uyghurs arrested, especially if the country in question was Muslim. Although he had never been to Turkey or the Arab countries, and had learned those languages on his own here in Urumchi, Adil worried that he was in danger.

Our conversation turned naturally to acquaintances who had been arrested. Adil mentioned that for the last month he'd been sleeping with a set of warm clothes by the head of the bed, and I told him I had been doing the same. According to Adil, a fair number of his friends and acquaintances were likewise sleeping with sets of warm clothing ready to go. Joking about the grim absurdity of it all, the two of us laughed for a moment.

FIFTEEN

The Door Closes

My sleep grew troubled. At night I tossed and turned between rest and wakefulness. My knotted thoughts faded into strange dreams. Although I got out of bed quite late, my body constantly felt heavy and tired.

One day I woke up around nine. I was still groggy when the phone rang, but when I saw it was Güljan I snapped into alertness as if a bucket of cold water had been poured over my head. For the last several months, simple phone calls like this had summoned people to their local police station or neighborhood committee, from which they were then packed off to "study."

Güljan told me that Marhaba and I had to report to the neighborhood committee in an hour. We must not be late. When I asked Güljan what the issue was, she must have sensed my nervousness. She assured me they only needed us to fill out a form. That was all.

Marhaba and I arrived at the neighborhood committee right on time.

It consisted of a large workroom, with doors leading to several small offices. I was familiar with the committee chief's office as well as the neighborhood policewoman's office. Most committee cadres worked at desks on one side of the large room. Only a few people were there when we arrived.

Güljan was waiting for us. She called over Adile, our neighborhood policewoman, who handed us four copies of a form with "Population Information Collection Form" written across the top in Chinese. Adile told Güljan that these forms needed to be completed immediately and accurately. Then she vanished into her office.

I had heard about this form. Practically everyone in Urumchi had filled it out since early April. People said the form prepared the ground for the mass internments that began later that month. It was widely believed that the form's data was fed into the notorious Integrated Joint Operations Platform. Over the last couple of months, several people had asked me whether I had filled out the form and had been surprised to learn I had not. I didn't know why this form had been presented to us so late, but there was no use now in wondering.

Güljan led us to a big table in the center of the office. "To save time, let me help you. I'll fill out the forms for the two of you, and each of you fill out a form for one of your children. I already have your basic information; I'll ask you for whatever I don't have." She explained to us which parts of the form we should fill out and which parts the authorities would complete on their own. Sorting deftly through the materials in the blue binder she always carried, she quickly located our family's files and began filling out the forms.

I looked carefully through the form. Employing the concision of Chinese characters to the fullest, the form was so crowded even the margins were in use. There were six sections: Basic Information, Movement Tracing, Religious Belief, Passport Holding Status, Stability Status, and License and Vehicle Status. Within each section was a series of small blanks, each more fateful than the next. It was clear that this form was targeted at Uyghurs.

At the top of the upper right margin, under the heading "Labels of Interest," five categories were packed vertically into a list: "person of interest," "member of a special group," "relative of individual in custody," "relative of suppressed person," and "marked in Integrated Joint Operations Platform." Marks could be made in the brackets following each category.

Below this, under the label "Key Information," was a further vertical list of nine categories: "Uyghur," "unemployed," "possesses passport," "prays daily," "received religious education," "has visited the twenty-six countries," "excessive time abroad," "possesses contacts abroad," and "school dropout children in household." Each category was likewise followed by a pair of brackets for marking.

Anyone could see at a glance that a person's political credit was determined by the fourteen categories under "Labels of Interest" and "Key Information." Each check mark inscribed in the brackets after these categories lowered an individual's political credit and pushed him one step closer to danger.

At the bottom of the right margin, under the heading "Type of Person," were three categories: "reliable," "average," and "unreliable."

Each of these was followed by a pair of brackets. Summarizing all of the data on the form, these three categories were the document's most important point. Rumor had it that people with a check mark next to "unreliable" or even "average" were sent to "study." It was imperative that our family be designated as "reliable." Each blank must be filled in with caution.

"What is your religious belief?" Güljan asked suddenly, looking at me a bit oddly. She had come to that section in my form. "None!" I replied without hesitation. Marhaba glanced at me in surprise. "Our family does not believe in any religion," I added. Marhaba understood my intention and nodded her head quickly to express agreement, but could not bring herself to speak the words aloud. Although Güljan knew we were lying, she continued filling out the form without comment. Adile emerged from her office and walked over to us. She looked briefly over the forms we were preparing before heading back to her office.

"Have you been to any of the twenty-six countries?" Güljan inquired.

"Which twenty-six countries?" I asked in turn.

Güljan swiftly drew a sheet of paper from her binder and handed it to me. On it was written in Chinese, "The twenty-six countries linked to terrorism are: Algeria, Afghanistan, Azerbaijan, Egypt, Pakistan, Kazakhstan, Kyrgyzstan, Kenya, Libya, South Sudan, Nigeria, Saudi Arabia, Somalia, Tajikistan, Turkey, Turkmenistan, Uzbekistan, Syria, Yemen, Iraq, Iran, Malaysia, Indonesia, Thailand, Russia, and the United Arab Emirates."

In other words, any Uyghur who had visited one of these twenty-six

countries was suspected by the Chinese state of involvement with terrorism. To the Chinese government, terrorism stemmed from these
countries. "Last year when we visited Europe with a tour group, we
passed through Turkey," I said, trying to play down our time there.
"That still counts," Güljan replied curtly without raising her head from
the form. Such arrogance was typical for Communist Party cadres and
police officers, but I was a bit surprised at this sudden demonstration by
Güljan, who usually came across as gentle and a bit shy. I felt deflated.

Once the forms were filled out, Güljan read them over carefully.
Then Marhaba and I signed them.

By the time we left the neighborhood committee office, it was already noon. We began walking home. "Forgive us, Lord," Marhaba
whispered.

With the world darkening around us, we did our best to find small moments of happiness for our family, and especially for our daughters.

On a fine Saturday afternoon, at Aséna and Almila's request, our
family went for a stroll at Tengritagh, a park that had only recently been
opened near our house. Once we had passed through the security check,
we could see there weren't many people around. This had been a neighborhood with a large migrant population; some had been arrested, while
others had been ordered back to their hometowns.

The newly planted trees were not large enough yet to provide shade,
and the park felt parched under the sun's glare. Even so, our daughters

were enjoying themselves. Marhaba and I likewise felt our spirits somewhat lifted.

While we were wandering around the park, we ran into an old acquaintance who had also come with his son for a stroll.

"Huh, is everything still all right with you?" he asked with a grin the
moment he saw me. "Have they not taken you to 'study'?" He knew I
had spent time in prison. I shuddered.

"Not yet." I maintained my composure with a joke. "I guess I'm not
qualified to go 'study.'" He had touched on our greatest fear.

He must have realized at once that he had said something inappropri-
ate. He needlessly informed us that he had come with his son for a walk
in the park, and then hurriedly took his leave. Marhaba's face had
clouded over. She was furious. Even the small pleasure of our walk in
the park had been ruined.

The next afternoon, I was sitting in my office, lost in thought. Grief
and anxiety about Kamil's arrest were still eating at me.

My cell phone rang. When I saw that it was Adile, I sprang nervously
out of my chair. My worry was not unfounded: Adile informed me
that our family—my wife, Marhaba, my daughter Aséna, and I—must
turn over our passports to her the next morning. Her tone was adamant.

The day I had dreaded, the day I had hoped would never come, had
finally arrived.

Our passports, with their ten-year American visas, were our only
passageway to freedom. As the mass internments edged ever closer to
us, losing our passports meant this passageway would be sealed shut.

We were crushed by the news. "Why?" Aséna asked in frustration. "Why are they taking our passports away?" She broke down crying.

"They gave us the passports, they can take them away whenever they want," I said, mostly to myself.

That night I was completely unable to sleep. After the mass internments began, word from the south was that those who had been abroad were among the first to be arrested. All passports were confiscated. I had worried endlessly about whether these policies would be implemented in Urumchi as well.

In late May, through an acquaintance, I had contacted a young Uyghur policeman who worked in the city police department's household registration bureau. I took him to dinner at Urumchi's most famous kebab restaurant. Over skewers of oven-baked lamb, I asked whether he had heard any chatter about passports being collected in Urumchi. He told me he hadn't heard anything like that, and that it was possible that passports would not be confiscated here. His words had put me somewhat at ease, and we had continued with our travel preparations.

Our plan had been to leave for America during the summer vacation. We had purchased four tickets—round trip, as we needed to persuade the authorities that we would be returning. The Chinese government we were trying to escape couldn't bear the thought of our abandoning it for the United States, while the American government that had grudgingly granted us visas didn't want us settling in the United States, either. It all made us wonder what we were worth.

Since our travel dates were at the height of tourist season, the tickets had been quite expensive. We had spent a significant part of our savings to acquire the passports and the visas. If our passports were taken now, the losses would be considerable. But that was just money. The real loss was that our passageway would now be closed, our hopes extinguished.

I had to find a way to keep our passports.

Looking at the problem from every angle, I eventually decided that traveling to America for medical care would be our most convincing and effective pretext. Still lying in bed in the dark, I started searching on my cell phone for information on Chinese citizens seeking medical care in America. Something caught my attention: numerous Chinese parents of epileptic children bring their kids to the United States for treatment.

That was it! Epilepsy, epilepsy with nocturnal seizures! That would be a good excuse, I thought. If we told the police we were traveling to America to have our older daughter, Aséna, treated for epilepsy, and that we had already purchased the plane tickets, we might be able to keep our passports.

We could say that Aséna's epilepsy flared up at night, and that to prevent people from gossiping, we had kept it from everyone, even our relatives, and arranged for her to be treated privately. In Uyghur society, people tend to keep medical matters private, and neurological and psychological ailments carried a certain stigma. People might believe us.

I was excited to have a plan. Feeling some measure of relief, I closed my eyes. Amid the vast darkness, a light now glittered.

In the morning, I told Marhaba and the girls about my idea.

"I have to get sick again?" asked Aséna. She was recalling the time three years earlier when we had invented a problem with her left ear, enabling her to stay home from school for a year and study English.

"We need you to make this sacrifice for our family's freedom," I said with a smile. I opened my arms. "Come here, my brilliant girl."

Aséna snuggled into my embrace. I stroked her skinny shoulders.

"Fine, then," she said. "If I have to be the sick one again, I will."

Marhaba was hesitant. "Will they believe us if we say that?"

"We have to try," I said emphatically. "If we don't offer some kind of reason, we might as well sit here and accept our lot."

Around ten that morning we called Adile. She told us she was taking care of some police business in the neighboring apartment complex, and that we should come meet her there. Marhaba and I walked over. This neighboring complex was attached to ours, and a majority of its residents were likewise Uyghurs.

A mass meeting was in session in the complex's public square, on the topic of maintaining stability in urban neighborhoods. Around three hundred people were in attendance, clearly residents of the complex summoned by the neighborhood committee. Nearby stood representatives of local government organs as well as neighborhood committee cadres. Passersby would stop briefly and look with curiosity at the proceedings.

Flanked by cadres, a Han official was speaking rapidly into a microphone. As we passed by the crowd, we heard someone remark in a low voice that the speaker was the deputy mayor. The local police were providing security at the meeting, and were standing at twenty- or thirty-meter intervals around the square.

This was where we found Adile. In despondent tones, we told her we had planned to go to the United States in July to seek treatment for our daughter Aséna's illness and that we had already purchased tickets. We implored her not to take our passports. Adile told us that collecting passports was an order from above and that no one could do anything about it. She added, though, that she understood our situation, and that after early July—considered a sensitive period ever since the Urumchi violence of July 2009—we could prepare medical verification of Aséna's illness and try applying for our passports back.

In other words, the light of hope had not yet gone out completely.

"How about the passport of our younger daughter, Almila?" I asked Adile. As soon as the words left my mouth, I realized what a fool I'd been to ask this question. "We've already notified everyone on our list this time," replied Adile confidently. "If she's not on the list this time, she might be on the next list." On our way home, Marhaba really let me have it over asking that question.

In the month leading up to mid-July, I sought out practically everyone I knew who worked in Urumchi's hospitals. When that proved insufficient, I spoke with the doctor acquaintances of our close relatives and friends. Of course, if I told them I needed a physician's confirmation of my daughter's illness in order to get our passports back, they would all be too afraid to help. "Passport" had become a frightening word. Numerous people had been taken to the camps simply for having one. Some Uyghurs had been so scared that they had voluntarily turned in their passports to the police or the neighborhood committee without even having been asked. Those who had never applied for passports boasted that they had been right in not applying, that in permitting Uyghurs to get passports the government had merely spread its nets to catch more fish. I therefore employed the vague excuse that "my daughter needs a doctor's note for school."

There's a saying in China: "A problem that money can solve is not a problem." I eventually found three people willing to help me for a price. One was a neurologist, the second was a brain scan technician, and the third was a hospital administrator. We needed the services of all three in order to acquire the necessary verification. Finally, after parting with quite a bit of money, we had the documents we needed.

In mid-July, I met with Adile. Less than a month after they began confiscating passports in Urumchi, the police authorities had prepared special forms for those applying to get their passports back. I filled out the forms, attached our one-page request letter and the medical documentation, and handed the papers over to Adile.

By late July, I had grown increasingly anxious as time passed with no word from the authorities. When I tried to read, my thoughts scattered, and I would be forced to read a sentence over and over before closing the book in frustration. When I attempted to watch a film, my eyes would be turned toward the screen but the movie would pass me by. The jumbled thoughts in my head could make no room for it.

I called Adile to ask where things stood. She told me that these issues were handled by a Han policeman named Zhang at the district police department's national security unit, and that I would need to call him and ask. When I called Zhang at the phone number she gave me, he informed me that a directive had been issued: no one with a history of foreign travel could get their passport back. My application had therefore been refused.

I felt sick. All of our work had been pointless. There was nothing for us now but to abandon all hope of leaving the country and await our fate.

Body

After exile water

after stray gatherings

after utter collision

after strange embraces

after bonding like ice

after infinite grinding

after silently rolling

after all the damn polishing

and

after fruitless forgettings

in the end

the grains of sand turned to stone

SIXTEEN

The Apartment

After the mass arrests began in Urumchi, Marhaba and I had decided that to be prepared for any eventuality, we should sell our apartment. With everything in such chaos, we knew that any sale would not be quick, so we hired a nearby real estate agency to sell the place. The wait began for someone to make us an offer.

Around that time, Marhaba's cousin Reyhan and her husband, Ismail, visited our apartment, telling us they had something important to discuss. Those days, the words "something important" were enough to worry anyone.

Reyhan and Ismail had lived in Urumchi since their marriage ten years before, purchasing an apartment and working in the clothing-export business between China and Central Asia. Their household registration, however, remained in their hometown, Ghulja. People without Urumchi registrations were being driven out of the capital, but they had heard that if you bought a home in Urumchi, the real estate company would move your registration to the city. Being registered in the capital, they thought, would provide them some safety. They had decided to pool all of their assets and purchase a second apartment, and they wanted our advice.

"To my knowledge, Urumchi registrations were frozen last year," I told them. "You can transfer a registration out of Urumchi, but you can't bring one here."

Ismail replied like a typical businessman. "Tahir *aka*, you're an intellectual. You think about things in terms of principles. But money can solve a lot of problems."

"Fine, let's say you move your registrations to Urumchi. They're arresting people here, too."

"Things are terrible in Ghulja; Urumchi is a good deal safer. The wind hasn't touched any of our friends in Urumchi."

In truth, they had not come to us for advice, but in hopes that we would accompany them and translate for them while they looked for apartments. Marhaba insisted that we help. Finally, I agreed to go with them and try.

The next day, the four of us headed to the new developments north of Urumchi and began making the rounds of some high-rise buildings. Although they were still under construction, units were already being sold.

At each building, a Han director would warmly greet us, and an attractive young woman would be assigned to show us a model apartment. We would begin by examining the unit's layout and size, then we would ask which floor the apartment was on and what kind of sunlight it got. Only then would we inquire as to whether they could transfer our registration to Urumchi if we purchased the apartment. On hearing that question, the young woman would immediately bring us back to see the director, who would tell us they could transfer registrations for those who purchased units, but that he would have to confirm the matter with the local police department. He would promise to call us the next day. Even as he was telling us this, it would be clear from his face that it wouldn't work out. In an exhausting week of rushing about, the same scene repeated at four different apartment sales offices. Just as I anticipated, not one of them called us back.

Unwilling to give up, Ismail had me call the first director who had promised to contact us. The director explained that with things so strict, the police were extremely busy, and he had been unable to get in touch yet with anyone at the station. With that, he concluded the conversation. Not a trace remained of the enthusiasm he showed on first meeting us.

Reyhan and Ismail finally admitted defeat. The four of us sat slumped on our living room couch. "I guess we'll see what becomes of us," Ismail said. Then, surprising us all, he burst out, "No matter what it cost, if I could I'd change our legal nationality to Han!"

The three of us stared at him. We'd heard of late that some Uyghurs were talking of changing their official nationality to Han. I figured that some people said this in all seriousness and others ironically. All of them, though, spoke from the desperation of the powerless.

Normally, it would be unimaginable for a Uyghur to say such a thing. I had seen Uyghurs who had married Han, Uyghurs with close Han friends, Uyghurs who looked down on their own people, and even self-hating Uyghurs, but before the mass internments I had never seen or even heard of a Uyghur who intended to shed their Uyghurness entirely and become Han.

When Ismail saw our surprised, troubled expressions, he hesitated a moment. Suddenly, he broke into a wicked grin. "Ha, you believed me!" We all laughed uneasily.

In mid-May, we met with prospective buyers for our home. They gave the impression of straightforward, hardworking people: a middle-aged couple from a village in the south who had worked in Urumchi as naan bakers for more than a decade. They had three children.

The real estate agency arranged for us to show them the apartment. When they arrived, Marhaba and I greeted them warmly. They followed us around the place, looking carefully and not saying a word. I could see from the woman's face that she liked the apartment, but didn't want to let on for fear we would raise the price.

It didn't take long to show them the apartment and settle on a price. Since our family was planning to go abroad soon, Marhaba and I didn't bargain strenuously, and we sold them the apartment below market value. Besides, the couple had spent more than a decade in this foreign city, baking naan and saving money, and their determination and work ethic impressed us. We even threw in the household appliances and furniture.

We signed a preliminary contract. They were to give us one third of the apartment price in cash, and the remaining two thirds once they obtained a mortgage. After three weeks taking care of various paper-work between the bank and the real estate agency, we went with the baker couple to the Urumchi Real Estate Management Bureau. The four of us waited in line for hours and signed a series of forms. All that was left was to sign the final document transferring the apartment deed to their name.

Just then, a Real Estate Management Bureau employee informed us that the Public Security Bureau would be investigating the baker couple's political background. The investigation would take thirty business days; only after the couple was approved could the deed be transferred. With that, all four of us began to agonize.

This was clearly a new policy; we had heard nothing of the kind from friends who previously sold or purchased homes. I turned to Marhaba. "It's over. All of our work down the drain."

The bakers were registered in their home village. Given that nearly all Uyghur migrants in Urumchi had already been sent back to their places of registration, it was surprising that the bakers hadn't been chased out of the city already. It seemed to me unthinkable that the police would grant them permission to buy an apartment in the capital.

As we left the service hall, Marhaba spoke to the bakers in a soft voice. "You haven't had any relatives arrested or locked up for political crimes, have you?"

"No, no one like that," replied the husband decisively.

"Wasn't that Dawutakhun of yours sentenced last year?" prompted his wife.

He contradicted her at once. "Dawutakhun wasn't sentenced for a political crime, he was sentenced for sending his son to a religious school."

Hearing this, I put a quick stop to the debate. People were bustling past us; if one of them heard all this, we might have a problem.

Marhaba and I resigned ourselves to the idea that the bakers wouldn't be able to buy our apartment. Having come this far, though, there was nothing to do but wait.

A month and a half later, the real estate agency informed us they had received word from the Public Security Bureau: the bakers had passed the political inspection! I smiled to myself in wonder. At a time like this, such luck was hard to believe.

Finally, we were able to complete the apartment-sale paperwork. Soon after, the bakers received the loan they had requested, and the remaining money for the apartment was deposited in my account. Our home had been sold.

While we had put our apartment on the market in case we decided to leave the country, our passports had been confiscated in late June while we waited for the police to complete their inspection of the bakers. With our apartment sold and our passports gone, we were as dazed as if we'd been chased out of our home onto the street. At Marhaba's suggestion, we reluctantly decided to find a new apartment.

Work at my company having come to a complete stop, there was little else to do. Marhaba and I began looking at newly built apartments in the vicinity. Meanwhile, we needed to rent a place.

Although Marhaba had lost all hope of recovering our passports, I wasn't ready to give up yet. I had a feeling that we could get them back.

For that reason, I insisted that we rent a home in the same complex we had been living in. If we moved elsewhere, we would be under the jurisdiction of a new neighborhood committee, and we might even have to transfer our household registration to a different police station. This would complicate still further any efforts to recover our passports.

We went to see several rental apartments, but none of them suited us. Then a Uyghur woman who ran a store in the complex recommended another apartment.

The next day we went to see the place. The owner was a Uyghur woman of about forty-five. Her two-bedroom apartment was rather nicely decorated, and was furnished with a bed, a sofa, and all the usual household appliances. She told us that she owned several apartments in Urumchi, that she had decorated this one with newlyweds in mind, and that no one had lived there yet. From the look of the place, she was speaking the truth. We liked the apartment. I joked to Marhaba that if we rented it, we might feel like newlyweds.

From her appearance, I would have guessed that the landlady was a civil servant. Most of Urumchi's Uyghur civil servants, though, would be hard pressed to purchase multiple apartments with their salary. Marhaba asked the woman what she did for a living. She replied that she was a businesswoman, and complained that the worsening political situation had been bad for business. She had therefore spent the last couple of months with her son in Canada, where he was studying. But the neighborhood committee back in Urumchi kept calling her, and she was forced to return. The day before yesterday, immediately after she got back, she had turned her passport over to the police.

"All because of those overseas splittists!"

Marhaba and I were briefly at a loss for words. "Splittist" was the word the Chinese government used to attack Uyghurs who wanted an independent state. While Uyghurs used the term when required to at government functions, they did not use it among each other.

"The kingpin of the splittists was arrested in Italy. I hope he gets what he has coming to him!" The businesswoman grew still more heated. "We all pay for their pointless actions!" She angrily jerked the curtains open. Marhaba looked at me.

"Which leader was arrested?" I was curious.

"That damned Dolkun Isa!" she spat, as if speaking of an ex-husband following an acrimonious divorce. Dolkun Isa was the general secretary of the Munich-based World Uyghur Congress. I later learned that he had been briefly detained by the Italian police while attempting to attend a conference in Rome.

Following the businesswoman's tirade about the splittists, we lost all interest in the apartment. So as not to give ourselves away, we made a show of looking around the place a bit more. "It's slightly small," we finally said, "and the rent is a little high. We'll give it some thought." We headed outside.

The woman was somewhat surprised at our sudden loss of interest in an apartment that a moment ago we had very much liked, but I didn't get the impression that she realized why we had given up on the place. When we took our leave of her, her face was still red with anger at the overseas splittists.

A few days later, we finally found a suitable apartment in our complex, belonging to a Kazakh merchant engaged in trade between China and Kazakhstan. The neighborhood committee, however, denied us permission to rent the place.

After the 2009 violence, many Han residents of Urumchi's old city moved to New Town, while numerous Uyghurs left New Town for the old city. Urumchi was becoming even more segregated than before. Not long after, the government adopted the "Integrated Settlement" policy: in neighborhoods where minorities comprised more than 30 percent of residents, no further minority individuals were permitted to buy or rent housing. The policy was intended to break up Uyghur communities and to scatter Uyghurs among the Han population.

After the neighborhood committee declined to authorize our apartment rental, we began asking around among friends and acquaintances for someone with connections at the neighborhood committee. Finally, we found a former classmate of the committee's deputy chief. This individual was a distant relative of Marhaba's, and he spoke with the deputy chief on our behalf. With great difficulty, we finally obtained permission to rent the apartment.

We paid six months' rent up front, then spent three days moving in. Aside from those things we would have immediate need for in the new place—pots and pans, dishes, clothing—we left our belongings packed up. We deposited the suitcases and bags in one bedroom, put the boxes of books and framed pictures in another bedroom, and made up the bed in the third bedroom for Marhaba and me. Aséna and Almila would sleep on the living room couch. In the middle of the living room, we piled big plastic sacks of bedding, plaster-wrapped dishes and crystal, and other items, unopened, just as we had carried them in.

After we finished moving out, Marhaba and I sank for the last time into the sofa we had given to the bakers, in the living room of our old apartment. Marhaba looked longingly around the place. Every corner of this home was filled with our family's memories. Leaving it, we knew we had come to a turning point in our lives.

SEVENTEEN

There Are No Goodbyes

Surrounded by anguish and uncertainty, I felt I was weightless, floating along the surface of time. I would spend hours on the sofa, my mind blank.

"I worry when you turn in on yourself like this," Marhaba would say. "Don't take everything so hard, it will all pass eventually. God will surely look out for us."

After our application to recover our passports was rejected, for a time I was busy looking for apartments. A couple of weeks had passed by the time I called Adile and asked to collect our application materials. There was no sense, of course, leaving falsified materials with the police. Adile told me she had taken the documents back to the station and that I could come pick them up.

"By the way," she added rather offhandedly, "we've gotten a new directive from above. Those with urgent business can now apply to have their passports returned to them. What would you like to do?"

I couldn't believe my ears. "In that case, we'll apply again." I spoke quickly, as if she might change her mind by the time I finished my sentence. "If you could be so kind as to help us once more."

"Summer vacation is almost over," Adile noted. "Will you have enough time?"

My response was firm. "Our daughter's health is more important than anything else. We'll make it in time."

Hope flickered into view once more.

The next day I went to Adile's office. I filled out the form requesting the return of our passports and handed it to her. Now all we could do was wait.

Rather than just marking time, Marhaba suggested, we should take a family trip to her hometown, Ghulja. I wanted to stay in Urumchi, though, and await news on our passports.

Marhaba encouraged me to accompany her. "If our passports are going to be returned, they'll call us. Can't we just head home the moment we hear from them?"

"You never know with them," I replied. "If they called to say we could come get our passports, it would be entirely possible for the policy to change again by the time we returned from Ghulja. So I'll stay here." Once they heard I wouldn't be going, my daughters decided to stay home as well. Marhaba left for Ghulja on her own.

The days felt endless. My daughters and I ate mostly in restaurants. Marhaba usually forbade Aséna and Almila from eating too much spicy food; now, with their mother out of town, they exploited my soft heart and ate their fill of their favorite fried, peppery dishes.

The daily routine of eating, sleeping, and eating grew ever more tedious. Aside from meals, Aséna and Almila didn't leave the apartment.

In those days of listless waiting, I began to take ever more frequent walks through the neighborhood to Almas's store after dinner. Since Almas had opened his convenience store a couple of years earlier, several close friends and I had regularly gathered there to chat, and would purchase this and that to support Almas. His store's business had been consistently disappointing, though he was certain it would improve.

When I went by the store, I would often find Almas seated at a table across from the entrance, translating Bertrand Russell's *History of Western Philosophy* from Chinese to Uyghur, his red "Security" armband on his sleeve.

Around that time, Almas got to know Mekhmut, a Uyghur officer in the local Public Security Bureau's National Security Detachment. One time I saw Mekhmut sitting and chatting with several friends in Almas's store.

Almas was pleased by his friendship with Mekhmut, even a bit proud of it. When I asked him what good could come of befriending a state security officer, he replied that it would "come in handy." I'll never forget the sly smile on his face when he said this.

Almas had good reason for this belief. In recent years, more and more people had been making friends with party officials or police officers for personal gain or as a kind of insurance policy.

One evening in mid-August, Almas and I met up at his store with three of our other closest friends. The five of us spent the night talking. Our conversation was deeply distressing.

All of us were shaken by the mass arrests that had continued since March. In particular, there were whispers of Uyghur intellectuals being arrested one after another. At that point it was impossible, though, to know what was true and what wasn't.

When we heard someone had been arrested, we would invariably ask what the reason had been. Each time we asked the question, though, we realized immediately how absurd it was. We knew perfectly well that the vast majority of the arrests were based on fabricated crimes. We all lived in fear, aware that we could be arrested at any time, on any pretext.

With everyone smoking constantly, the air in the one-room store grew hazy, and every little while we would open the door to air out the place. Afraid that passersby would overhear our conversation, we always quickly pulled the door shut again. If a customer walked into the store, we would halt our conversation until they left.

We talked for about three hours.

"I wish the Chinese would just conquer the world," one of my friends said suddenly.

"Why do you say that?" asked one of our companions.

"The world doesn't care what happens to us," my first friend replied. "The world doesn't understand China. Since we can't have freedom anyway, let the whole world taste subjugation. Then we would all be the same. We wouldn't be alone in our suffering."

"It's looking like you'll get your wish," said a third friend.

As always, our conversation that night reached no conclusions, and we reluctantly prepared to head home simply because it had gotten late.

We didn't gather to solve the problems confronting us, but to exchange ideas and share our burdens.

There is a Uyghur custom that when a parent dies, people pay visits to the bereaved. Each visitor will ask the host how their father or mother died. The host will patiently relate the very same account to each guest. The more this is repeated, the more the host's grief will subside. Our conversations in Almas's store were like that. Lately it was as if we were addicted to sharing our troubles.

When we all left Almas's store that night and said our goodbyes, I pulled my friend Perhat Tursun aside. At a quiet corner of the building, I told him that Kamil had been arrested. Although I had promised Munire that I would speak of this to no one, Perhat was a close friend of Kamil's and mine, and I felt that he should know.

Perhat registered no forceful reaction. Seeming at a loss for words, he only wrinkled his face in sadness. "My God, what is it that you're saying?" he intoned softly. The news had been a further blow to a man already in pain. We both fell silent.

"Did you drive here?" I asked, changing the subject.

"No," he replied, looking to the dark side of the street. I figured he must have counted on our drinking tonight. Although no one was really in a drinking mood today, we had bought a couple of bottles of red wine from the store so as not to sit there empty-handed.

"Come on, then, let's flag down a taxi for you on the main street." I gestured for him to walk with me to the road.

"That's OK, I'll walk home through these back streets."

"What for? It will take you an hour to get home on foot."

"Someone told me I should keep away from people right now, so that no one informs on me. I'll take the back streets. These days, aside from going to work, I barely go outside."

"Why would anyone inform on you?" I couldn't help asking it, but as soon as the words escaped my lips I realized once more what a pointless question it was. We were living in a time when it was absurd to ask why.

"All right, then. Take care!" I held out my hand to him.

Since we saw each other frequently, we didn't usually shake hands on parting. Perhat hesitated for a moment. Then he half-heartedly extended his hand. It felt cold and lifeless to the touch.

This might be the last time we ever saw each other, and I wanted to hug my dear friend tight. But I could not.

With his head cocked slightly to the side, as was his habit, he walked quickly in the direction of the back streets. I watched as his figure faded into the black.

That evening, as we parted ways in front of Almas's store, I dearly wished to say a heartfelt goodbye to each of my friends, but I had to suppress the desire. If we could get our passports back, the journey before us would be a one-way trip. It was clear that if I made it to America I would request political asylum, and in doing so become an enemy of the Chinese Communist Party, an enemy of the state. Experience told me that if the police learned any of my friends had known I would be going abroad or had said a final goodbye to me, they would be in trouble: at the very least, weeks of interrogation; if they were less lucky, the camps. I couldn't let my friends face that danger on my account. If I left, I would have to go without a word.

The second time we applied to have our passports returned, I felt optimistic about our chances. Marhaba suggested that our family head to Kashgar to bid my parents farewell. Much as I longed to, though, out of caution I had to decline.

According to my mother, the neighborhood committee had installed a camera by the front door of each apartment in her complex. The residents had to pay for the cameras; my parents turned in 280 yuan to the neighborhood committee to have a camera installed in front of their door.

These cameras monitored the people entering and exiting each apartment. Since a fair number of people were needed to watch so many video feeds, the neighborhood committee hired a bunch of young lowlifes from the neighborhood at a minimal salary. Fancying themselves policemen, they took to the job with relish.

Practically everyone in my parents' complex knew I had spent time in prison. If we visited my parents' apartment, the goons monitoring their apartment camera could recognize and report me. Or someone at the neighborhood's mandatory nightly political meetings could fulfill their denunciation responsibilities by informing on me. My parents and I would be in trouble.

Two decades earlier, when I was twenty-six, I had not told my parents I was planning to go abroad to study. Following my arrest at the border and three years in prison, I had returned to my childhood home in Kashgar.

One day, my father and I were sitting on the summer bed in the court-yard, sipping tea while yellow grape leaves drifted down from the trellis above. Suddenly he spoke. "My child, a person embarking on a long journey should have his parents' blessing first."

I couldn't swallow my tea. I wanted to sink into the earth with shame.

However proud my parents had been that I attended college in Bei-jing and found a good job as a teacher, they were just as heartbroken when I was arrested, imprisoned, and deprived of my position for a rea-son they could not understand. I was so chagrined to hear my father's words that I promised myself I would never again leave for a long jour-ney without bidding my parents farewell.

Yet this time, likely the final time, I was once again leaving without saying goodbye to my mother and father, without their blessing.

In this life, perhaps it is my fate to leave those closest to me with no goodbyes.

EIGHTEEN

A One-Way Journey

The days crawled past as we waited for the police to contact us about the passports. Making it from morning to evening was a constant challenge.

One afternoon I headed out again around six. My attention was drawn to three men, two Han and one Uyghur, sitting and smoking on a bench in front of our building. When my daughters and I had gone out for lunch around noon, I had seen the same men sitting on that bench. Even then, something about their appearance had made me suspect they were plainclothes policemen. Now that I saw them still sitting there, my suspicions hardened.

After an hour's walk, I returned to the courtyard and saw the three of them still sitting on their bench. This time, I decided to walk discreetly by them to get a closer look. As I passed, I noticed a bulge at the waist of the man sitting closest to me. The butt of a pistol peeked out from a half-open holster under his white shirt. I shuddered. It felt as if they had been sent just to monitor me. Hiding my unease, I walked quickly by.

I called Marhaba the moment I was home. Not daring to broach the topic over the phone, though, I contented myself with asking briefly how she was doing. I said nothing to my daughters, either. That evening I sat sleepless till midnight, my mind filled with thoughts and speculation. Once the hour passed twelve with no knock at the door, I grew a bit calmer. Still, I slept in my clothes.

The next day, as soon as I got up, I walked outside to see if the policemen were still there. They were gone.

A few days passed. On Tuesday, I got out of bed around nine. My whole body was stiff, and I was fatigued, as if I had been performing heavy physical labor.

I headed over to the living room. All our belongings from the old apartment were piled crazily in the middle of the floor. A depressing sight.

Aséna and Almila slept sweetly on the couch. I didn't even feel like washing my face or eating breakfast. I slumped into a chair and began scrolling through WeChat groups on my phone.

My phone rang. It was Marhaba, calling from Ghulja.

"What are you up to?" She sounded in high spirits. Spending time with family and friends in her hometown had clearly been good for her.

"I'm just sitting around," I replied dully.

"And the girls?"

"They're still sleeping."

"No news from the police?" she asked.

"Nope."

"I got a call," she said. "They told me we could come get the passports."

"What?" I had to make sure I hadn't misheard her.

"They're returning our passports."

"Don't joke."

"I'm not kidding, it's true!" I could hear the excitement in Marhaba's voice.

Aséna raised her head from the couch where she had been sleeping. "Dad, are they giving the passports back?"

"Yeah!" I couldn't hide my delight.

Hearing all this, Almila was now wide awake, too. The two of them jumped up and down on the couch and yelped with sheer joy.

"Go pick them up right now," said Marhaba. "I'll send you the number of the officer who called me. You can pick up the passports at the new City Administrative Services Building. Oh, and don't forget your ID card."

"OK, I'll head right over. And you get going, too—take the train back today. If there's not a train, take a plane!"

Barely stopping to wash my face, I told Aséna and Almila to eat breakfast and hurried out to the car.

"Dad, drive carefully!" Aséna called after me. "Don't let all the excitement get you into an accident."

"God forbid," I called back. "Don't tempt fate!"

My car was parked in front of the building. I started the engine and sped down the road.

The main hall of the administrative services building housed service centers for city government offices. I walked into the Urumchi Public Security Bureau's service center and told the policewoman at the counter that I'd come for our passports. She directed me to an office, where a middle-aged Han policewoman sat looking at her phone. I explained why I had come. After taking my ID card, she picked up a register book from the table and searched for our names. She found them on the third page, and then carefully compared the name on my ID with that in the register. At her request, I signed my name next to my entry.

Opening a drawer packed with passports, the policewoman extracted one and handed it to me. It was Aséna's. I told the officer that we had applied to have three passports returned. She informed me that only one passport had been approved.

I was beside myself. "Please check again," I pleaded. "We applied for three passports so that we can have our daughter's illness treated abroad."

The policewoman grudgingly rose and located our application materials in the cabinet that held the passports. Returning to her seat, she looked carefully over the first of our file's more than ten pages.

"You're right, it's three passports," she muttered. "Why did they only write one in the registry?"

Thank God, I said to myself.

She opened the drawer of passports again. Checking the numbers in our application materials against the numbers pasted to the passports, she quickly found the remaining two passports and handed them to me. Taking the three passports, I thanked her profusely and left the office.

It was a miracle.

I had barely walked a few paces from the office before I heard the policewoman calling nervously.

"Hey! Hey! Is that your bag?"

I wheeled around to see that the policewoman had already hastened out of her office. She looked frightened, as if there were a bomb in my bag. In my excitement, I had forgotten it in her office.

Apologizing to the policewoman, I returned immediately to the office, picked up my bag from the chair, and walked out.

"Is there money in the bag?" joked a Han policeman at the service counter, having watched all of this.

"I've got no money," I replied. "I've just got my life."

I didn't even think to put the passports in my bag, instead clutching them in my hand as I headed toward the building entrance. Two Uyghur youths, waiting on a bench in the middle of the lobby, stared with mouths agape when they saw me holding the passports. It was as if they had seen a ghost, so fearsome had passports become for Uyghurs.

I walked out of the massive building with steps so quick I couldn't tell whether my feet touched the ground or not.

As soon as I was outside, I called Marhaba. She was at a friend's house. "Did you manage to get them?" She spoke in a low voice, careful not to let the people around her hear, but it wasn't hard for me to sense her deep excitement. I suggested she go somewhere she could speak privately. We decided we would leave in three days, and Marhaba began preparing to take the first train back to Urumchi.

Once I was back in the car, I called Li Yang. I told him we had gotten our passports back and asked him to purchase four tickets to America, departing in three days' time.

"Are you sure? I wouldn't want you to have to cancel the tickets and take a hit like last time."

"That's exactly why we need to get the earliest tickets possible and leave right away."

Li Yang knew that our passports had been taken away and that we'd been trying to get them back. He had helped us purchase our previous tickets to the United States, and when we'd had to cancel them he had felt bad for our lost money.

Li got back to me without delay: there was a flight from Beijing to Boston on August 25. I told him to buy round-trip tickets on the spot; we needed the return tickets for the sake of appearances. I also asked him to purchase tickets for us from Urumchi to Beijing for August 24. Today was the twenty-second. We had one day to make our preparations.

When I returned home, Aséna and Almila had finished breakfast. They were dressed in their nicest clothes, as if we were leaving today. Seeing how joyful they were, I knew that everything we had been through was worth it.

I took my daughters to our favorite Uyghur restaurant. We ate our lunch with gusto. It had been months since I had enjoyed a meal that much.

That night Marhaba's train arrived from Ghulja, and we went to meet her at the station. Standing by the exit, we could see even across the platform how happy she was. The two of us rushed into each other's embrace like in the movies.

This was an embrace not of meeting, but of celebration. Marhaba and I had never been in the habit of greeting each other with a hug. When they saw us, Aséna and Almila were embarrassed in front of all the people passing by. They teased us, grimacing.

Driving home, the four of us planned out the day and a half we had left, deciding the order in which we would take care of everything. Our family entered a state of high readiness.

The next morning I drove to a used-car dealership and sold our car without bargaining. Then I headed home to join in the preparations.

I felt that we should bring nothing but essential summer clothes, a few books, and some daily necessities. This was not for traveling convenience but to avoid anything that might arouse suspicion when we crossed the border. Chinese border guards would be sure to notice a Uyghur family that took an unusually large amount of luggage on vacation.

Marhaba, however, wanted to take as many of our belongings as possible. We grew heated as we debated how much we could take and which things we should choose. I could tell how crestfallen she was as she gazed at the cherished garments we had to leave behind. I knew she would be angry at me for a while over this, but I hard-heartedly stood my ground.

It had been sixteen years since Marhaba and I had started our family. Each of us was past forty, and our two girls were in their teens. Yet all we could take from our life together was packed into four suitcases and four little bags.

In another box, we gathered important items we couldn't take: four family photo albums, assorted letters and documents, my book and journal publications. The photos in the albums were our family's entire past. For Marhaba and myself, the photos from our youth were particularly meaningful. I labeled the box and left it for my cousin to send after us.

Early the next morning we called my in-laws and asked them to come over. When they arrived, we told them we were leaving for America today so that Aséna's illness could be treated. They knew perfectly well that Aséna wasn't sick, but they knew equally well how serious the political situation had become. They grasped immediately that for us to make it out of the country, we needed to hold fast to this pretext. We watched as their expressions turned from surprise to understanding to grief.

"But will we see you again?" asked my mother-in-law.

"Don't worry," I replied with more conviction than I felt. "As long as we're alive we'll meet again."

On the sofa, my father-in-law's head sagged. My mother-in-law looked longingly at Marhaba. Averting her eyes, Marhaba busied herself with zipping one of the suitcases shut.

Around noon, the taxi we had called stopped in front of our building. My father-in-law and I stuffed our suitcases into the trunk and placed our knapsacks on the back seat. My mother-in-law emerged from the building and fell sobbing on Marhaba. Fortunately, the courtyard was practically empty; still, I worried that tearful goodbyes might draw people's attention. With the excuse that we would miss our flight, I hurried Marhaba on. We urged her parents to return to the apartment without delay. Then we climbed into our taxi. Marhaba's face was still wet with tears.

We drove out of the gate and onto the access road in front of the complex. Along the sidewalk, people were passing this way and that. Among these Uyghurs, their shoulders bowed with worry and their daily toils, were people we knew.

"Are we going to abandon these kinfolk here?" Marhaba asked sadly. I glanced warily at the Han driver, but he gave no sign of knowing Uyghur. Brow furrowed, he was fully focused on the road.

A few days earlier, I had heard that police officers sent from Xinjiang had been stationed at border control in the Beijing airport, specifically to monitor Uyghurs leaving the country. As we sped down the outer ring road, I called Adile to tell her we were on our way, and to ask her what we should do if the police stopped us at customs in Beijing. She told us not to worry, that if we had any issues we could contact her.

We arrived at the Urumchi airport. The atmosphere inside was tense. At the entrance and in the terminal, armed special police scrutinized the people passing through, especially Uyghurs.

After dropping off our luggage and collecting our boarding passes, we headed to the security checkpoint. I was standing first in line, and when I emerged from the checkpoint, two Han security officers led me over to a separate room for further inspection.

Inside was a jury-rigged conveyer belt that orbited a pillar. I was told to stand atop the conveyer belt and hold my hands up high as it carried me around the pillar, which appeared to be scanning my body and sending readouts to a computer nearby. There had been no such inspection at this airport when we'd traveled to Beijing the previous year.

Having completed the process, I exited the room. Marhaba and our daughters were likewise obliged to undergo this additional inspection. While waiting for them, I watched Han passengers pass through the conventional security check and hurry off to their gates. The security officials paid them no mind. *This extra inspection is just for Uyghurs,* I thought with renewed humiliation.

The security inspections finally came to an end without further incident. We walked over to the gate and sat by the window. There was still time before boarding; Aséna and Almila wandered off to stretch their legs.

Watching the planes on the runway through the enormous windows, I turned to Marhaba. "Take it all in. These may be our final moments in this land."

"Don't say that." Her voice was trembling. "God willing, we will return." As soon as the words left her mouth, she started weeping. "God willing!" I whispered. Tears were rolling down my cheeks as well.

Our plane left the gate right on time. Marhaba and I sat next to each other; Almila and Aséna took the seats directly in front of us. While the airplane gathered speed on the runway, Marhaba looked forlornly out the window. I realized that her right hand was gripping my left hand tightly, as if holding on for dear life.

As the aircraft lifted into the sky, I felt my heart sinking. It was a sensation unlike any I had experienced. We were losing our homeland.

In a low voice, I told Marhaba to look as we passed Boghda Mountain. She displayed no reaction as she stared out the window. Standing alone in the distance, the snow-capped peak gleamed in the sun.

We landed that evening at Beijing Capital International Airport. After putting our suitcases in storage, we took a taxi to the Xinjiang Affairs Complex and checked in to our hotel rooms. We were exhausted from our travels and from two days of anxious scurrying. Barely had we checked into our rooms than we were fast asleep.

The next morning we woke our girls from their slumber and made a perfunctory breakfast of naan we had brought from Urumchi. Then we headed back to the airport.

At border control, my turn came first again, and I handed my passport to the agent. The uniformed young officer opened the passport and looked long and hard at me, comparing my face to my passport photo. Then he motioned another officer over, this one wearing civilian clothing. I figured this must be the officer sent from Xinjiang. Leaning in close, they looked at the computer screen and spoke briefly with each other. Then the plainclothes officer left.

"Seems you've been to America before?" asked the border control agent. From the way he said it, I gathered we were considered more reliable due to having previously been to the United States and back.

"Yeah," I replied with a curt confidence implying I went to America all the time.

He stamped my passport and returned it to me. I had been approved to leave the country. Marhaba and our daughters likewise moved swiftly through the process.

Soon we were in the air. I felt a heavy weight had at long last been lifted. I ached, though, when I thought of the loved ones we were leaving behind. The unknown future before us frightened me as much as it excited me.

"Dad, how can I study in American schools if I don't know English?" Almila looked back at me through the gap in the seats.

"You'll learn it once you arrive."

"What if I fall behind in my classes before I learn the language?" Her eyes grew moist.

"You're smart, you'll learn it quickly." I smiled at her.

"Don't worry," Aséna reassured her. "English isn't hard."

I found some comfort in that moment, thinking that at least my two girls would have a good future in America. Then I sank back into my seat and began thinking about the past. The time left until Boston would be enough to recall my whole life once through.

Seventeen hours later, the aircraft descended through the Boston sky and landed on American soil. We passed successfully through customs.

We were free.

At Logan Airport we bought tickets for the next flight leaving for

Washington. As we sat waiting to board, Aséna and Almila were riveted by the utter newness of our surroundings and the rainbow of humanity passing by. Marhaba sat beside me, sunk in thought. I knew what was preoccupying her. Every time I tried to imagine how we would start our new life in America, I found I simply couldn't focus. Even with a new world before us, my thoughts wandered constantly back toward home.

Somewhere Else

Besieged by these discolored words

within all these disordered moments

the target on my forehead

could not bring me to my knees

and also

night after night

one after another

I spoke the names of ants I've known

I thought of staying whole

by the road or somewhere else

Even

cliffs grow tired staring into the distance

But

in my thoughts I trimmed your ragged hair

with two fingers for a scissor

I splashed your chest with a handful of water

to douse a distant forest fire

Of course

I too can only stare

for a moment into the distance

Exile Dreams

I was running for my life. Half a dozen Chinese military police chased after me, fully armed, barely a step behind. But this was the neighborhood where I was born, with roads I knew like my five fingers. I skillfully evaded my pursuers, rounding corners as lightly as a bird, leaping nimbly as a rabbit over the low mud walls between houses. The police, though, stayed right on my heels. Just then, a siren sounded nearby. A police car careered toward me. My steps grew heavier. Now they would catch me for sure. The officers caught up with me and pressed me to the ground. I struggled with everything in me, but my arms and legs were pinned down. The police car's siren wailed ceaselessly.

I awoke with a start. My body was covered in sweat. Another nightmare.

An ambulance was passing by, siren blaring, in front of our apartment complex in the suburbs of Washington, DC—the police car from my dream.

From the day I arrived in America, I have had such dreams many times, in slightly different forms.

Not long after we settled in Washington, I dreamed of my mother several nights in a row. Uyghurs take such dreams seriously, and I began wondering if something had happened to her or if she was worried about me. I decided to call my parents to ask how they were doing. I imagined my cousin in Urumchi had already told them we had left for America. Even so, I needed to tell them with my own voice. They were both over seventy.

I knew the situation in Kashgar was grave. We had come to America with police permission, though, under the pretense of procuring medical treatment for Aséna, so I wasn't overly worried about calling my parents.

Over the phone, I told my mother that we had come to the United States to have Aséna's illness treated and that we would be staying here for a while. I talked a bit with my father as well. Reading between the lines, they both understood that Aséna's illness was a necessary fiction. They wished us good fortune, told us to return once Aséna was well, and warned us to keep our distance from bad people and bad things. By "bad people and bad things," they meant people and situations the Chinese government disapproved of. I promised my parents we would stay in touch, and we said goodbye.

The next day, my brother in Kashgar left me a voice message on WeChat. Two hours after my phone call to my mother, national security agents had come looking for her. They confiscated her cell phone and ID card for having received a phone call from abroad. My mother was terrified.

My father and brother went to the national security unit headquarters. They told the officers that it was I who had called my mother; that in fact my parents had already made a clean break with me; that they had long ceased even considering me their son; and that in the future they would have absolutely no contact with me. After my father and brother signed a document guaranteeing all of this, they were able to recover my mother's cell phone and ID card.

I could hear the anger and disapproval in my brother's voice. He finished his message by asking us not to contact them again.

In early October, I received an unexpected phone call from the baker couple who had purchased our apartment in Urumchi. It was the husband's number. I figured he might be calling about some minor issue with the place—the electricity, the water, the gas. I was pretty sure he didn't know we had left the country; if he had known, he wouldn't have dared to call. Not wanting him to run into trouble on my account, I didn't pick up.

Just a couple of weeks later, though, we were deeply distressed to learn from my cousin that the baker had been sent to a concentration camp. Afterward, Marhaba and I spoke often about how his wife and their three children might be faring, and wondered how she was managing to pay the mortgage. Every time we discussed it, Marhaba's voice would grow sad and dispirited. "May God have mercy on them."

Right around then, word came that Ismail, husband of Marhaba's cousin Reyhan, had been summoned to Ghulja and sent to "study." Reyhan and their two young girls were left in Urumchi. Marhaba cried for days.

When we left Urumchi, I had carefully labeled that box with the photo albums and other precious items. I left it in our apartment, intending to ask my cousin to send it after us once we arrived in America. In the empty days while we were waiting to get our passports back, I had even visited Urumchi's central post office to ask whether packages could be sent to the United States and about the costs involved.

After arriving in America, we were busy for a couple of months setting up our lives. In October, I left my cousin a voice message on WeChat, asking him to send the albums. My heart sank when I heard his response.

"Almas has left to study and it looks like my turn will come soon. This is the last time I'll be in touch. Take care of yourself." His voice was lifeless. It seemed Mekhmut, the state security officer in whom Almas had placed high hopes, hadn't come in handy after all.

From the tone of my cousin's reply, I knew that another wave of mass internments had begun. I sat there on the couch, phone in hand, staring at the wall. I felt myself sinking into the white wall's blankness.

By the end of October, having realized we would not be returning to Urumchi, the police searched the home we had rented from the Kazakh businessman. Then they sealed the door. We didn't know what they were looking for or whether they took anything from the apartment. We learned, though, that the apartment remained sealed until the middle of the following year, placing the landlord in a difficult situation.

The landlord had rather good connections in Urumchi, though, and with the help of various friends and acquaintances he persuaded the police to remove the seal. The apartment was his again. Perhaps our relatives had a chance then to remove our belongings.

In November, my cousin, Marhaba's two brothers, and Arman were arrested and sent to "study." The police sought out my cousin's wife and Marhaba's sister-in-law and questioned them about me. Our distress grew ever deeper. We were tortured by the thought that our relatives might have been arrested because of us.

Once they realized we had left the country, relatives and friends began deleting Marhaba and me from WeChat. For their safety, we likewise decided not to communicate with anyone back home. All direct contact with our homeland was now severed.

As soon as we had enrolled our daughters in school, Marhaba and I began attending English classes at the neighborhood center. After so many years, I had once more become a student. No matter how hard I studied, though, I felt like nothing stuck. While the teachers were speaking, thoughts of everything happening back home would flood into my mind.

When I was ten, my parents sent me during winter break to study with the imam at the neighborhood mosque. Back then, religious instruction was still permitted. Nearly all of the neighborhood kids studied a month or two with that imam. They would learn the Arabic alphabet, memorize some important and frequently used verses from the Quran, and learn how to say the five daily prayers.

On the first day of lessons at the imam's house, I sat with four other boys my age, clustered around the stove. The imam cleared his throat. "Learning in childhood is like engraving in stone," he began. "Learning in old age is like writing on sand."

Now I was seeing the truth of what the imam had said. The verses I learned from him all those years ago are still crystal clear in my mind. Now that I was older, though, I was feeling ever more keenly my diminishing ability to learn new things. Concentrating was a challenge amid so much anxiety.

Four months or so after arriving in America, I began having somewhat different dreams. I would be standing at border control, preparing to leave China, when police would arrest me and rip up my passport. I would wake up howling.

In early 2018, the American anthropologist Darren Byler traveled to the Uyghur region to witness the mass internments that had been underway for a year. He had previously lived in Urumchi for a time, during which he was on good terms with Almas and other friends of mine. Now, arriving in Urumchi, he wrote me without delay. I asked him to look into a number of friends, particularly several who had recently disappeared. Among those Darren tried to find was Almas. I drew a map of the street where Almas had his convenience store, marked the spot where the store stood, and texted Darren a photo of the map. He found the place I had designated, but the store was locked. It clearly had not been open for quite some time.

Not long after, word spread in the Uyghur diaspora that Perhat Tursun had been sent to a camp. No other details were forthcoming. I waited for further information, hoping that the reports were false, but in my heart I knew Perhat had been taken. This was one of the things I had most dreaded hearing. It turned out Perhat's efforts to avoid people had been in vain; there was no escaping the gaze of the party. From that day on, something scraped at me inside. The pain was deep and lasting.

Midway through the year, the American historian Joshua Freeman traveled to Urumchi. He had lived in the Uyghur region for many years, and wanted to see what was happening there with his own eyes. He went to a Uyghur bookstore on Unity Road that I knew well. To avoid drawing attention, Josh waited till he was alone with the shopkeeper. Then he began picking up books one by one from the shelf. Gesturing at each book's cover, he asked indirectly how each author was faring. "Is he around? Is she OK?" The responses were mostly the same. Very few writers were OK.

Finally, the bookstore owner asked Josh how I was doing. Josh told him I was fine. "What a lucky man," replied the shopkeeper. "He left at the right time."

Once I began to adjust to life in the United States, my dreams changed again. In these dreams, I would return from America to my homeland. With dear friends and family I would eat in familiar restaurants, stroll through lovely orchards, gather in broad courtyards to sing and feast and talk. I would tell them about America. But at precisely these joyful moments, the police would arrive and confiscate my passport. I would be overcome with pain, and would regret ever having returned. I would awaken, my heart aching.

Every time I awoke from one of these terrible dreams, I would see where I was and sigh with relief. Thank God, I would say to myself.

I would sometimes hear from other Uyghurs in the diaspora about the nightmares they had. No doubt there were even more dreams that I didn't hear about; many people don't pay much heed to their dreams, and are not in the habit of relating them to others. I myself never spoke of these dreams in front of my daughters; they were still adolescents, and I didn't want to upset them. I usually discussed my dreams with Marhaba, who would tell me that the same fears haunted hers: police chasing her and taking her passport, her closest friends abandoning her. "Our bodies might be here," she would say, "but our souls are still back home."

In the year since arriving in America, we had been living off the money we brought with us. As the Uyghur saying goes, though, "If you only sleep and eat, even a mountain won't last." Our savings were rapidly diminishing. After I received an American work permit in mid-2018, I began thinking about what work I could do until my English improved and I found a job that fit my skills. I decided to become an Uber driver, a common profession for Uyghur immigrants in the DC area. All one needed was a work permit and a car. Among the Uyghurs driving Ubers in America were former doctors, professors, jurists, engineers, and even government officials. I joined the Uber ranks in September.

I was encouraged to find that my Uber earnings were sufficient for our family's daily needs. Besides, I was restless after sitting at home for a year. Back in our homeland, I was used to working every day, and it was hard for me to simply stay idle. As I drove passengers to their destinations, my aching heart took some comfort from the attractive neighborhoods of northern Virginia, the mysterious back streets of the capital, the open roads of southern Maryland.

As I drove, I would lose myself in thought as I remembered my friends back home. I'd have long conversations with them in my mind. Sometimes I would forget there was a passenger in the back.

In March 2019, Marhaba told us she had had a strange dream: a small, spotted snake had found its way into our house. Although she was usually deathly afraid of snakes, this little snake didn't frighten her at all. Women who dream of snakes, she declared, give birth to boys. None of us paid this much mind until one night a couple of weeks later, when Marhaba informed us she was experiencing unmistakable signs of pregnancy.

The moment she heard this, Aséna shook her finger at us. "What have you two done?" she fumed. "It's dangerous for Mom to give birth at this age! My God, my God!" Following her older sister, Almila likewise wagged her finger at Marhaba. "I want a sister. If you give birth to a boy, I won't look after him!" She ran angrily upstairs.

In the middle of the night, Aséna and I picked up a pregnancy test at the drugstore. The test confirmed that Marhaba was pregnant. Noticing that I had fallen silent, Marhaba asked me what the matter was. "I never imagined this happening," I replied, remaining very quiet.

Twelve years earlier, the birth of our second daughter, Almila, meant that Marhaba and I had reached our government-allotted quota of children. The neighborhood committee ordered Marhaba to have a birth control device inserted in her womb. The IUD caused Marhaba serious abdominal and back pain, however, and she had it removed. Now, after more than a decade without conceiving, my forty-five-year-old wife had discovered she was pregnant.

You could call it a miracle. Aséna's worries, though, were not misplaced. Giving birth at this age carried significant risk. The primary reason I had fallen silent, though, was that raising a child would be extremely challenging at our age and in our present circumstances. After all of our work raising Aséna and Almila, we had only just begun to relax as they began building their own lives. In our homeland, relatives had sometimes helped take care of them, but in this foreign land we would confront every challenge entirely on our own. Uyghurs say that "children arrive with everything they need," but raising and educating a child is a major responsibility. It requires tremendous effort, care, and patience.

Marhaba was certain that she would give birth to a boy, as she had long hoped to. The thought delighted her. Since our arrival in America, I had often likened our family to an old tree forcibly transplanted from one patch of soil to another. Such a tree would produce roots only with difficulty, and might even waste away. Now Marhaba looked me in the eye. "Why can't you see that this child is our old tree's first root in this new soil?"

The next day we took Marhaba to the doctor. The baby was healthy. A month later, we went to the doctor again and learned that the baby would indeed be a boy, and that Marhaba was in good health. Rejoicing, our family declared Marhaba a specially protected member of the household and began preparations for a new member's arrival.

But in our American existence, joy and grief followed each other at a dizzying pace. As time went on, I felt more and more that our life was splitting into pieces.

Midway through that year, word came that Eli had been arrested and sent to a camp. Needless to say, Eli's bookstore, like most Uyghur bookstores in our homeland, was shut down by the government. As for Kamil, from the time we arrived in the United States I continually tried to get word of him but could find no reliable information on his fate.

Our son was born in mid-November 2019. With joy and excitement I took him in my arms: a precious gift for my fiftieth birthday. We named him Tarim, after the largest river in the Uyghur region. The majority of our people live in oases on the fringes of the Taklamakan Desert; most of these oases draw their water from the Tarim. Uyghurs call it the Mother River. We wanted our American-born son never to forget his motherland.

Every time I called my son's name, I would think of Perhat Tursun's poem "Tarim River." Silently, I would wish Perhat peace and safety.

Before long, though, I received grim news. In February, Josh Freeman and I were invited to give a poetry reading at Yale University.

While waiting in a department lounge for the event to begin, I received a voice message from a Uyghur poet in the diaspora, informing me that Perhat had been sentenced to sixteen years in prison. Josh and I sat there, at a loss for words. I didn't want to believe it.

Within a week, another acquaintance of Perhat's in the diaspora confirmed that he had been sentenced. For several days I walked around in a daze. Nothing got through to me. Finally, to make absolutely certain, I called the number I found online for Perhat's workplace in Urumchi. The Han woman who answered the phone listened silently as I explained that I was a friend of Perhat's, that I had been unable to reach him for quite a while, and that I wanted to know how he was. As soon as I finished speaking, she hung up without a word. When I called back, no one picked up. Only then did I truly believe that Perhat had been sentenced.

I found myself thinking of the first lines of "Tarim River." It was as if Perhat had written his own fate in that poem.

> Like the waters of the Tarim
> we began in this place
> and we will finish here
> We came from nowhere else
> and we will not leave for anywhere . . .

Uyghurs who had come to the United States earlier than us said it took three years for a Uyghur to adjust to life here. Before we knew it, four years had passed, and I did consider myself pretty well acclimated. There were moments, though, when I had trouble believing I was in America. Suddenly, I would feel that it had all been a dream. As if one day I would wake up in my Urumchi apartment and say to myself, What a long dream that was; as if I would then enjoy a leisurely breakfast with my family and drive my old Buick in the early-morning sun to teach my class at Xinjiang Arts Institute; as if by noon I would be with Eli in his bookshop, eagerly debating the newest Uyghur books; as if in the afternoon, I would take care of all the work that had piled up at my office; as if I would spend the evening with Kamil and Perhat and Almas, talking and laughing over beer and kebabs in Almas's convenience store.

In the months after my arrival in the United States, I was gripped by conflicting feelings of excitement and uncertainty, joy and pressure, anger and hope. My heart knew little peace. This was doubtless why I rarely found myself able to write poetry. Even in quiet moments, the verses wouldn't come. Instead, I would remember Munire sobbing, or Perhat hurrying off into the dark. Often, I would see in my mind's eye the torment of my dear ones. My cousin, weak and emaciated in his cell; Eli stooped over in an interrogation chamber; Almas undergoing political reeducation; Arman, forced to labor in a cotton mill; Ismail with a group of prisoners in the camp yard, shouting red songs of praise for the party in Chinese.

One autumn night a couple of months after our arrival, I had another dream. I had died. I lay on my right side, unable to move, while five or six of my closest friends stood around me. They looked on in lamentation, hands clasped, white mourning shrouds around their waists.

Sorrow and regret were written across their faces. I tried to cry out, "I'm not dead, I'm safe and sound in America," but I couldn't speak. I tried to move my limbs to show them I was alive, but my legs and arms wouldn't budge. I was terrified they would bury me alive.

The dream was as vivid as real life, and it troubled me for days. I couldn't get it out of my head. It was this dream that led me to write my first poem since escaping China. Once the dream was captured in verse, I felt somewhat lighter. But the feeling was fleeting.

Having escaped the terror, we are a fortunate family. Yet while we know the joy of those lucky few who boarded Noah's ark, we live with the coward's shame hidden in that word "escape." We are finally free, but those we love most are suffering still, left behind in that tortured land. Each time we think of them, we burn with guilt. We will see these dear ones only in our dreams.

What Is It

What is it

from far away, from behind the domed water,

that stayed with me, that came along with me?

A weak vow written in the yellowing fog,

audacity standing at an angle

or

the layered dimness passed from hand to hand?

These days

are crowded with shattered horizons,

shattered!

In the runaway season

when surrender hides deep in the suitcase

when noble doubts run over the weight limit

when dead ends continue onward

when the exodus stalls at the second floor

what is it

that keeps you from seeing I am still alive?

So simple are my inner soul and outer face,

oh dark-eyed one,

a tree that reddens from within

turns to stone beside me

A spray of sweet-smelling camel grass

grows quickly, blooms open

at the doorstep of the past

Acknowledgments

To begin with, I would like to offer special thanks to Joshua Freeman, whose contribution to this book has been far more than just the translation. Without Josh's support and encouragement, this memoir would likely never have been written. A witness to many of the events described in the book and well informed about others, he offered numerous helpful suggestions regarding the memoir's content and structure. He translated the book with remarkable conscientiousness and helped see it through the publishing process, and provided a heartfelt and moving introduction that will prove most helpful to readers in understanding the memoir.

Prashant Rao at *The Atlantic* played an indispensable role in the editing and publication of my article "One by One, My Friends Were Sent to the Camps," which laid the foundation for this memoir. I likewise want to thank Ellen Cushing and others at *The Atlantic* for all that they did to help make that piece possible.

I would like to express my gratitude to Chris Richards, this book's initial editor at Penguin Press. Chris encouraged me with his invitation to expand my *Atlantic* piece into a book for this venerable publisher, and provided valuable suggestions in the first stage of editing. After Chris moved on from Penguin Press, Emily Cunningham took up the role of editor, and with formidable skill and dedication offered innumerable edits and suggestions that improved the book. I am very grateful to her, and will not forget the many others at Penguin Press whose efforts helped bring this book into being. I likewise want to thank Bea Hemming and Jenny Dean at Jonathan Cape; they have been an important part of the editorial and publishing process from the beginning.

Sincere thanks are due to Adam Eaglin at the Cheney Agency. With the deftness of a seasoned professional, he has guided us through the publishing process with sincere and generous advice. Adam's colleagues at Cheney have contributed in many and important ways to the book's publication, and I greatly appreciate their continuing efforts to introduce the book in numerous languages and countries.

I want to express my profound gratitude and respect to Perhat Tursun. Our lifelong friendship is a constant source of pride for me, and the suffering Perhat is now undergoing has spurred me on in the writing of this memoir. My sincerest thanks are likewise due to those individuals described in this memoir whose names I cannot mention out of concern for their safety. What value this book has is inseparable from their unforgettable experiences. When the day comes that I can express my gratitude to them openly, I look forward to rectifying this situation and to thanking each and every one of them.